ART THERAPY COLORING

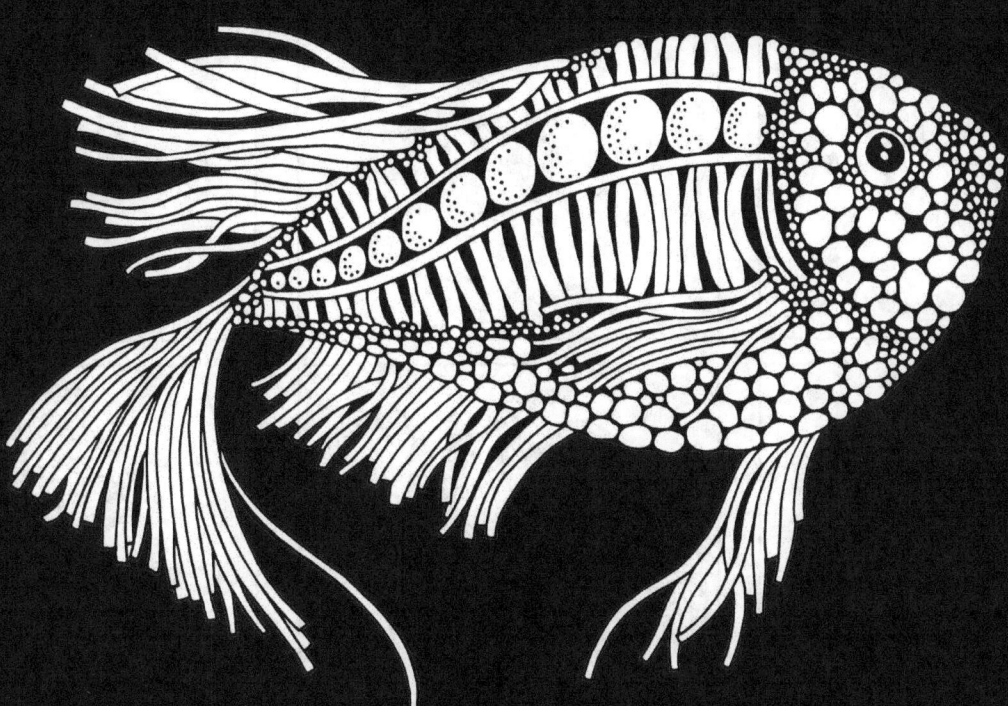

OCEAN
COLORING BOOK
FOR SENIORS MEN

Preview of Coloring Pages

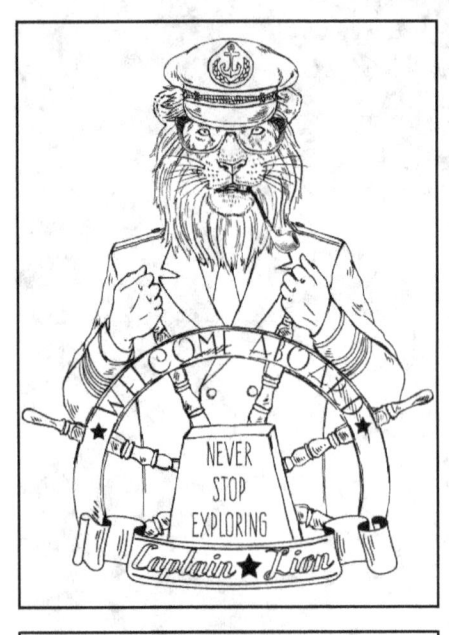
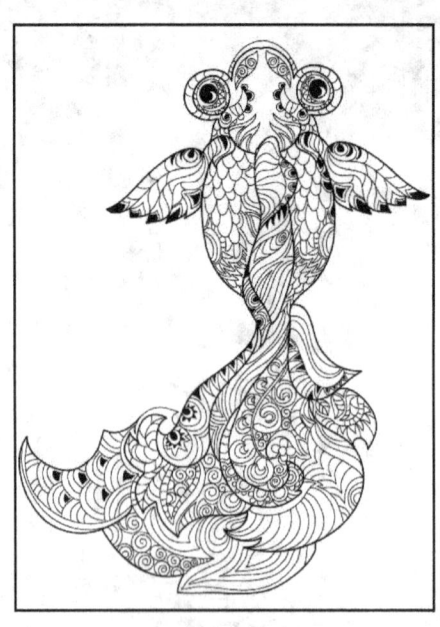
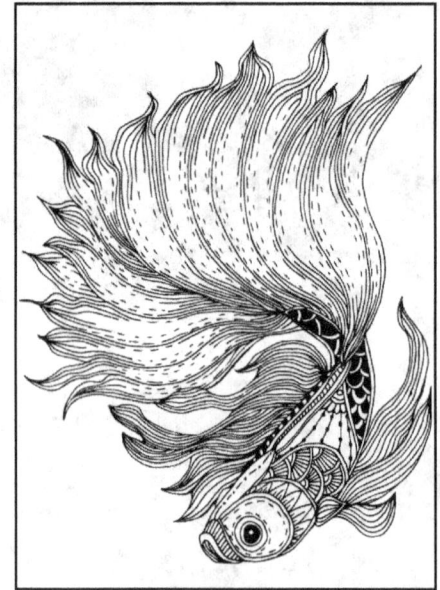
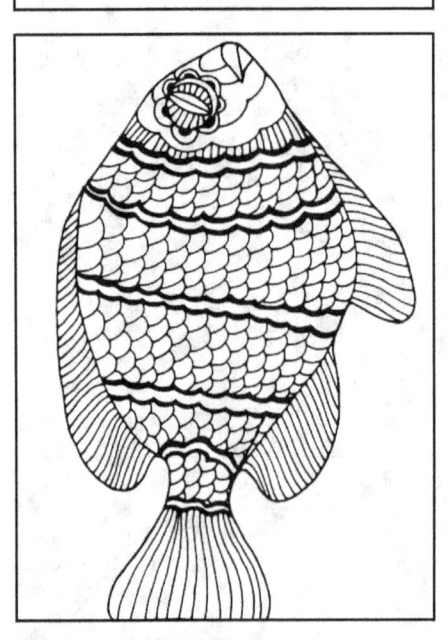
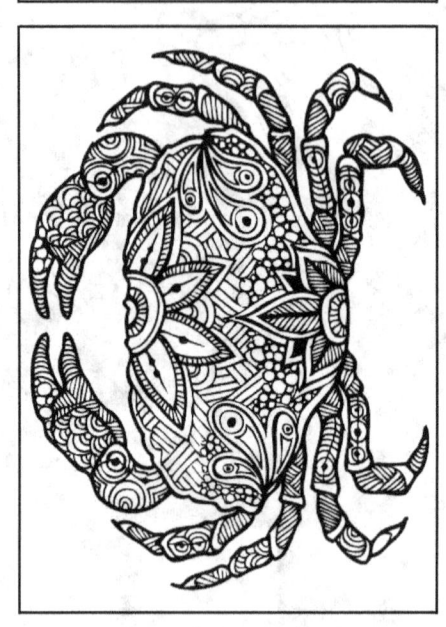
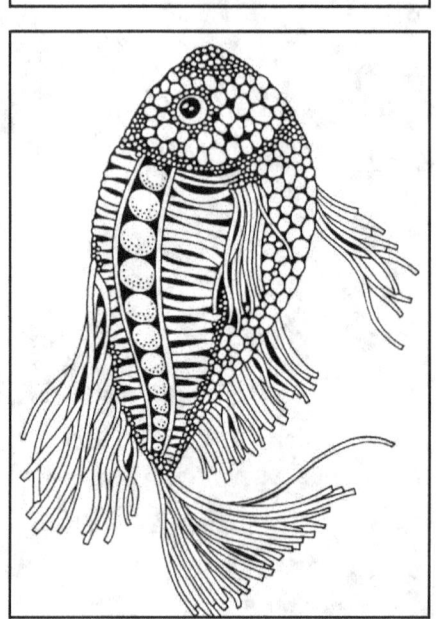
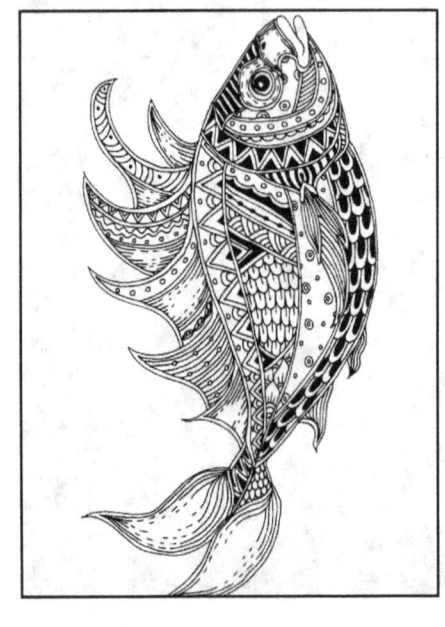
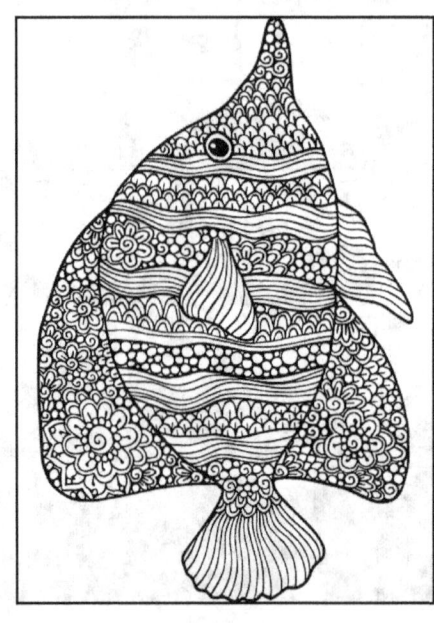
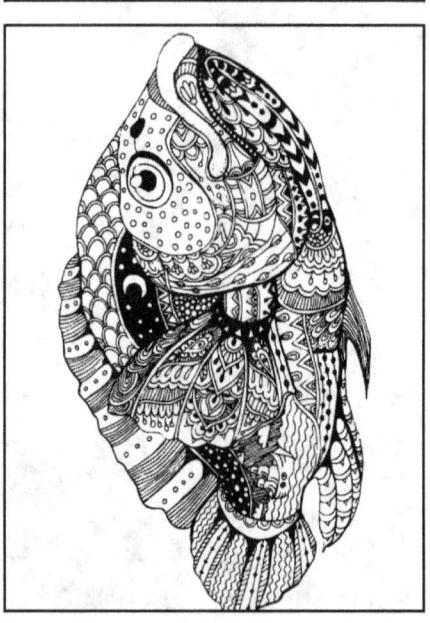

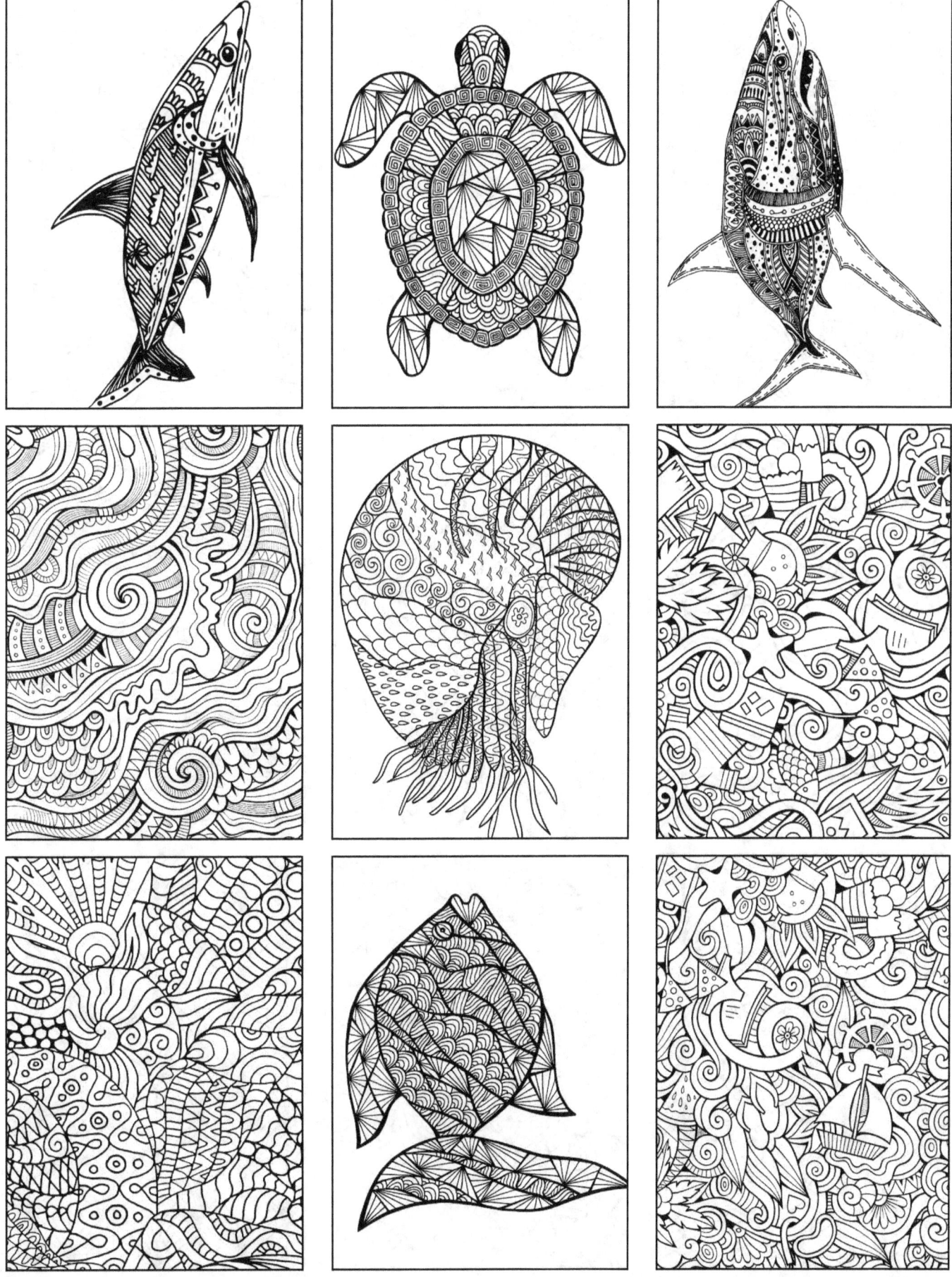

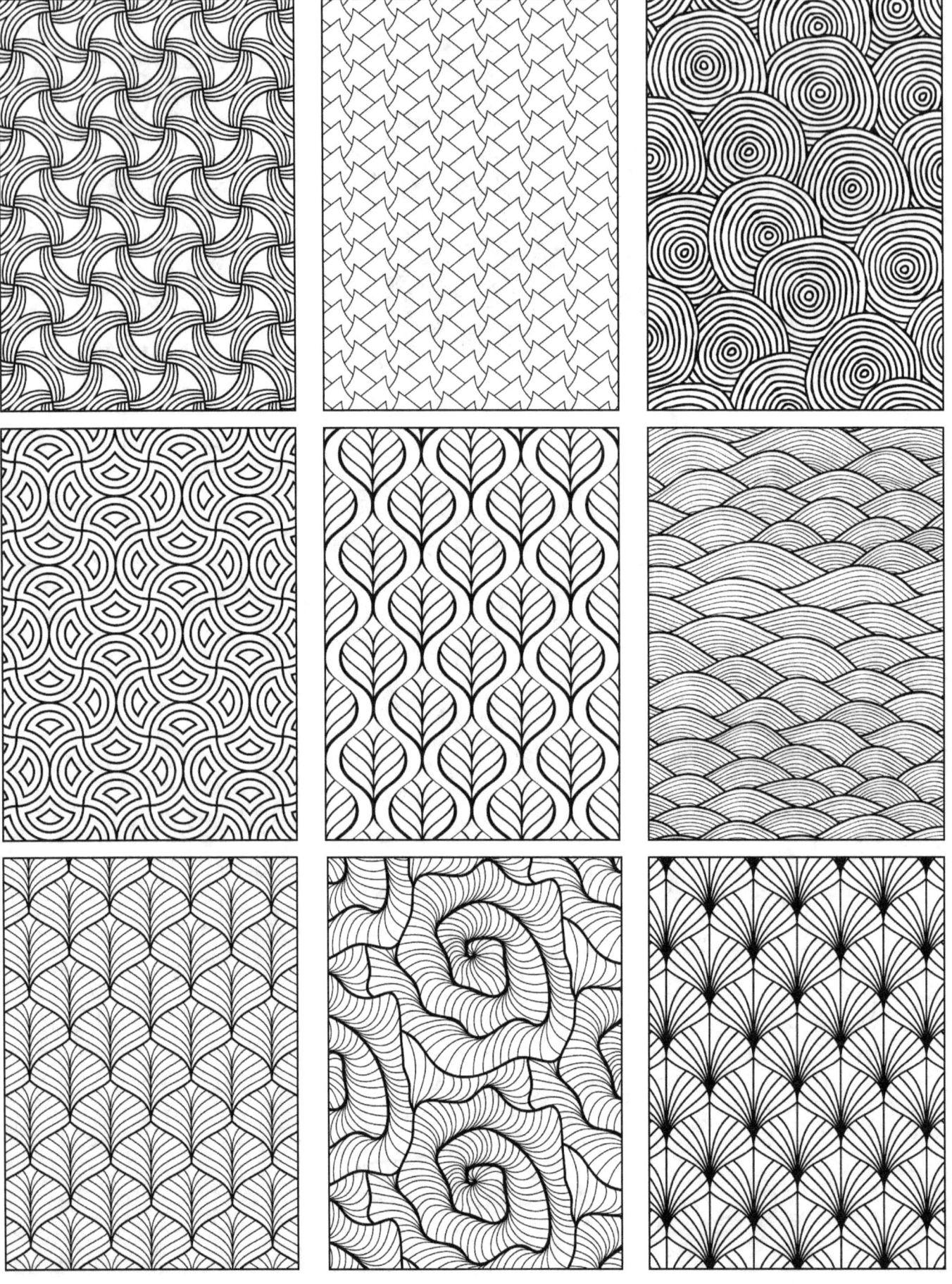

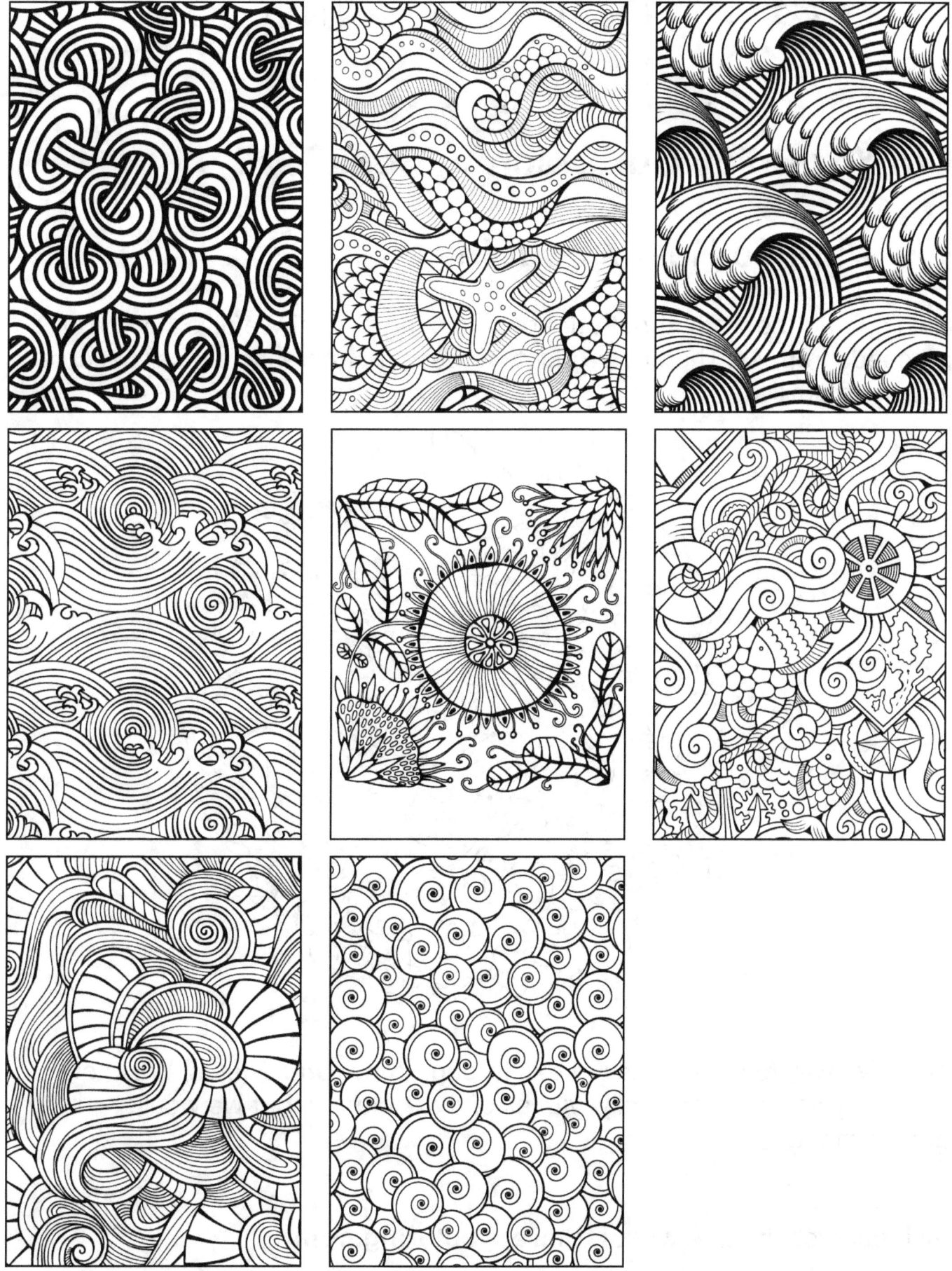

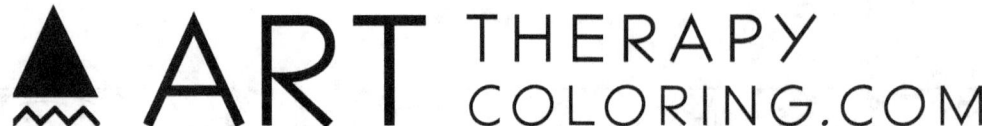

Did You Enjoy Our Coloring Book?

We Want To Hear About It!

Help spread the word about our adult coloring books! We give 10% of all proceeds from Art Therapy products to benefit pancreatic cancer patients and their families.

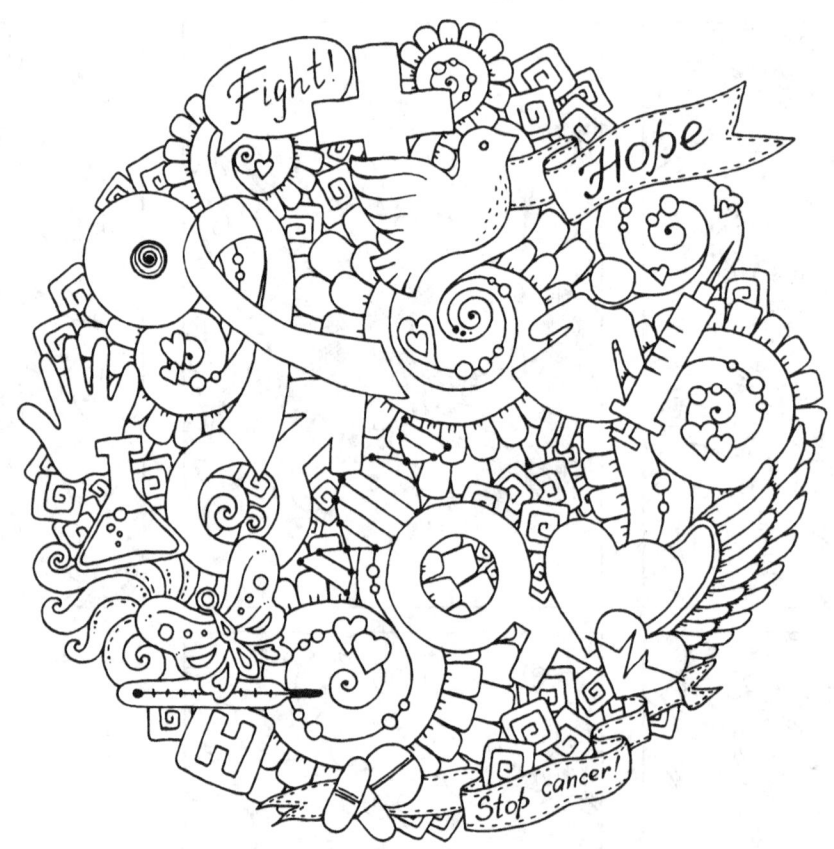

The best way to spread the word is through **Amazon reviews**. We know how busy you are, especially with all of that coloring, but we would appreciate it!

Visit our website at **www.arttherapycoloring.com**

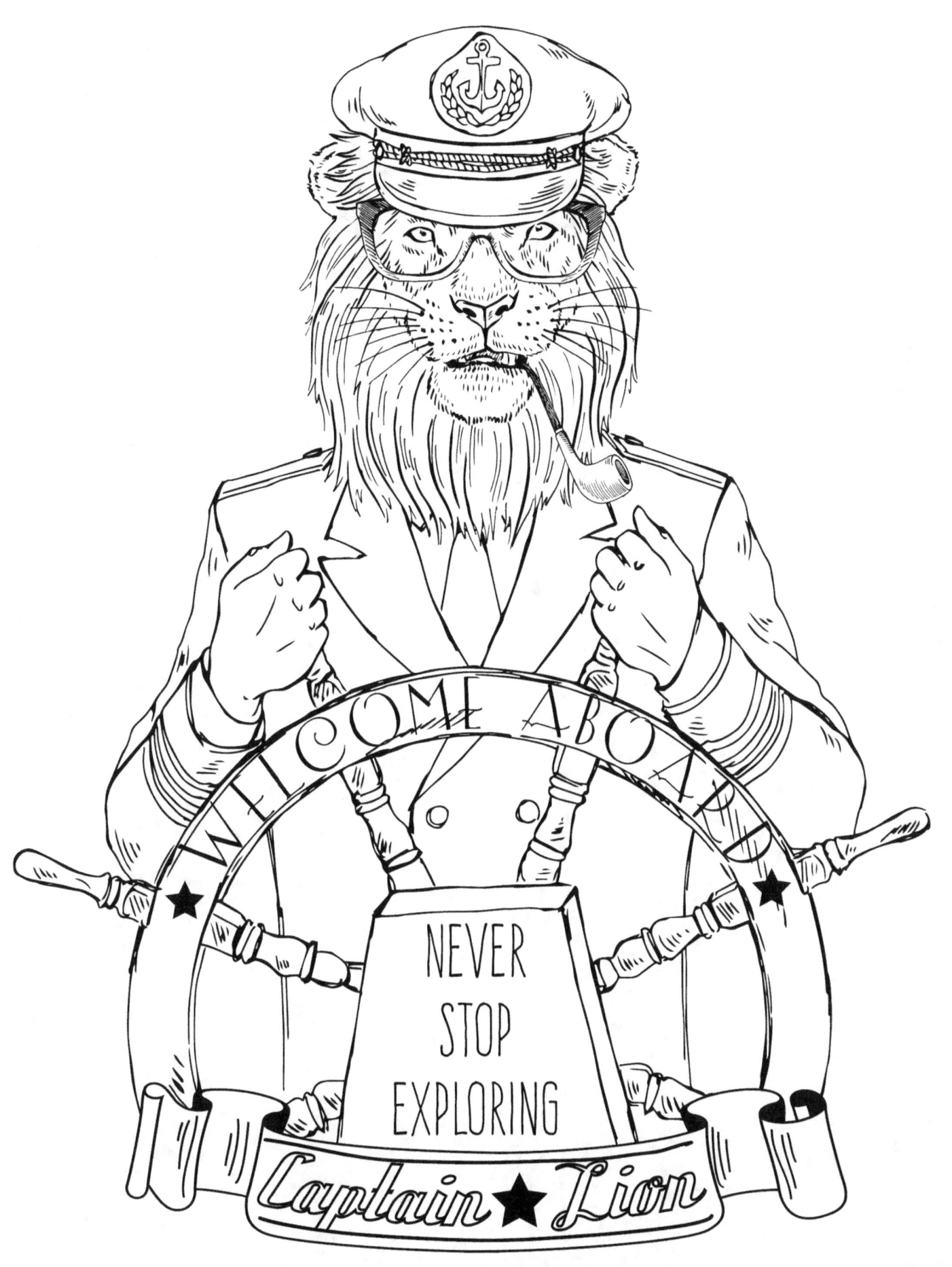

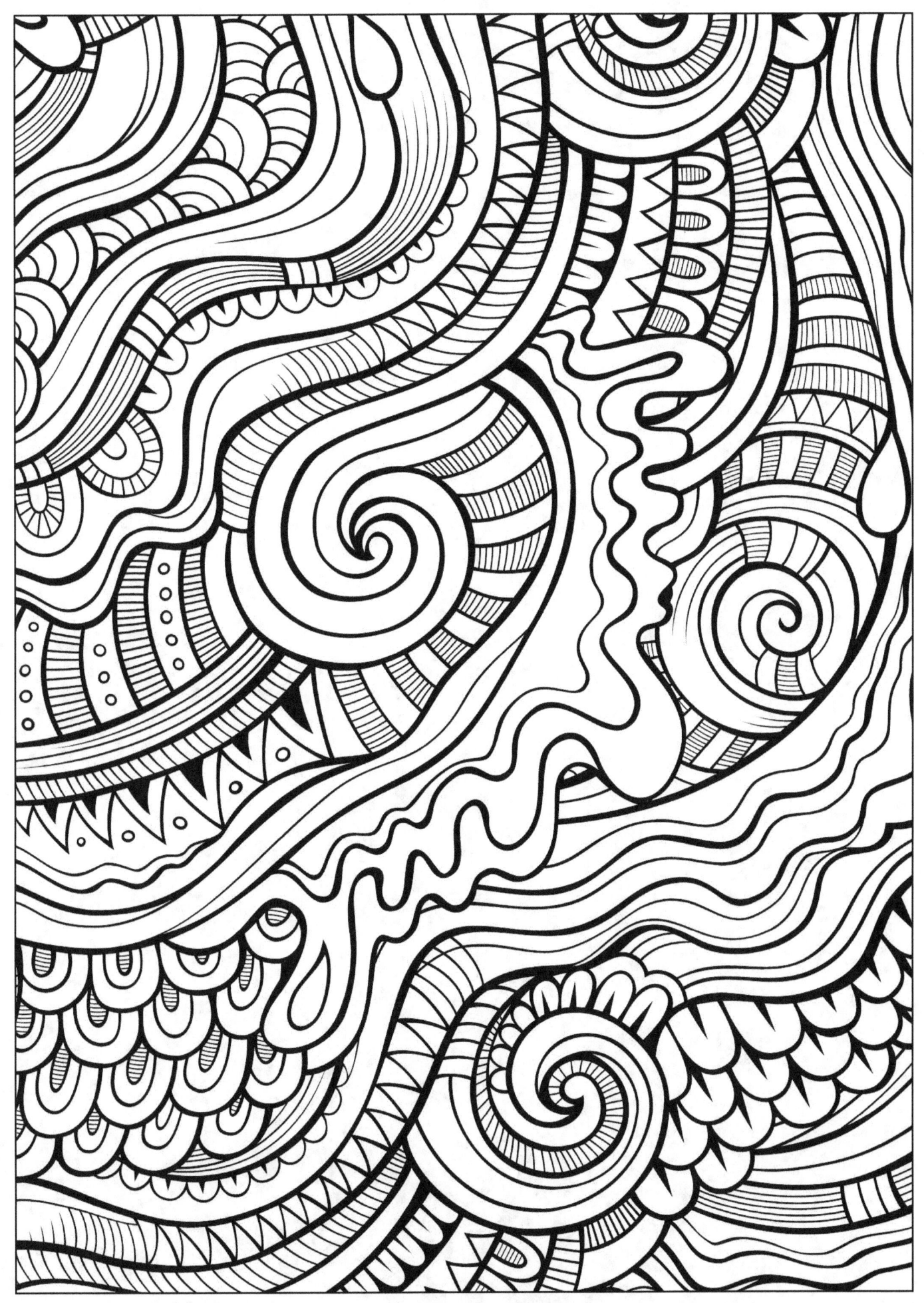

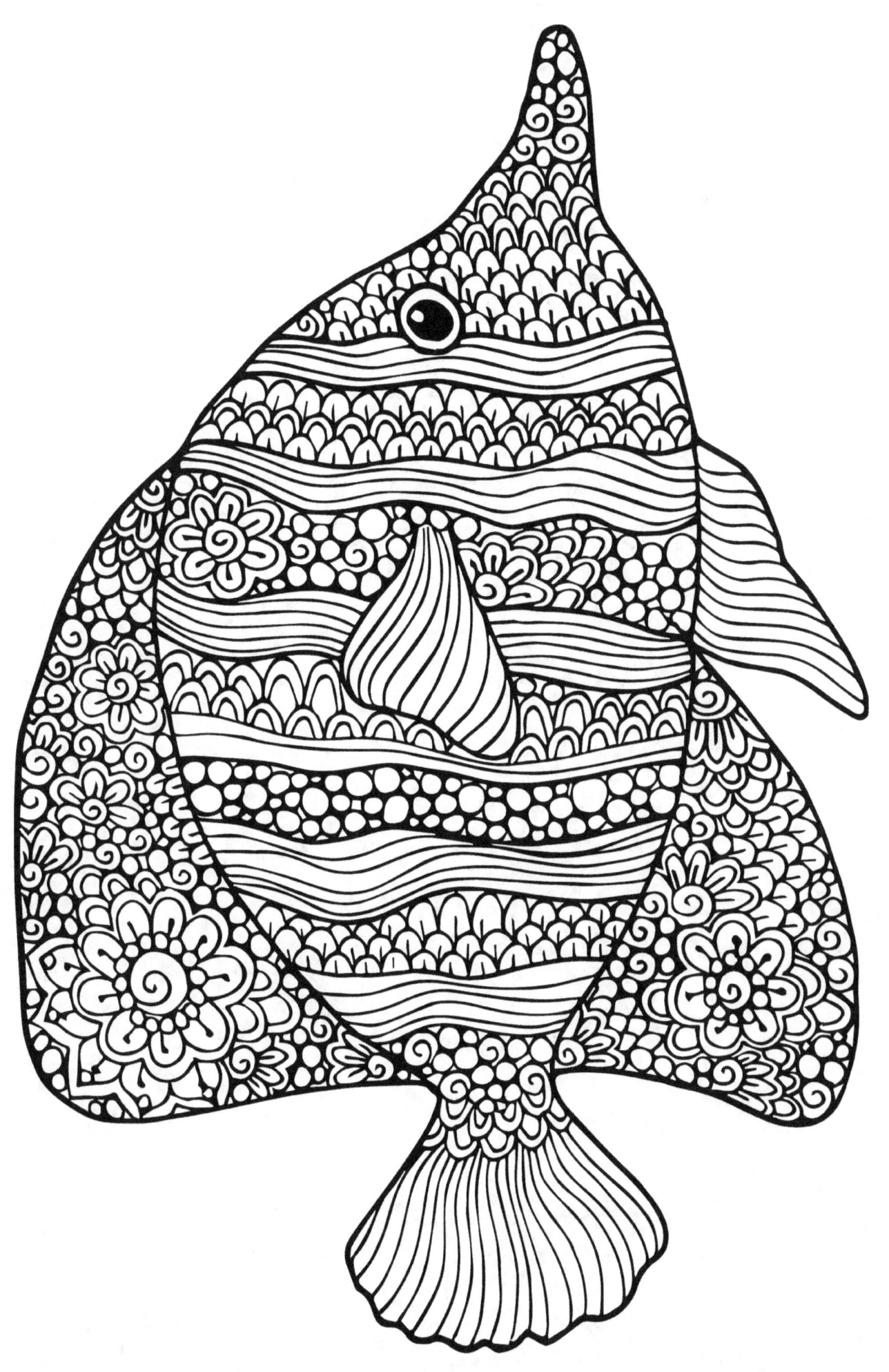

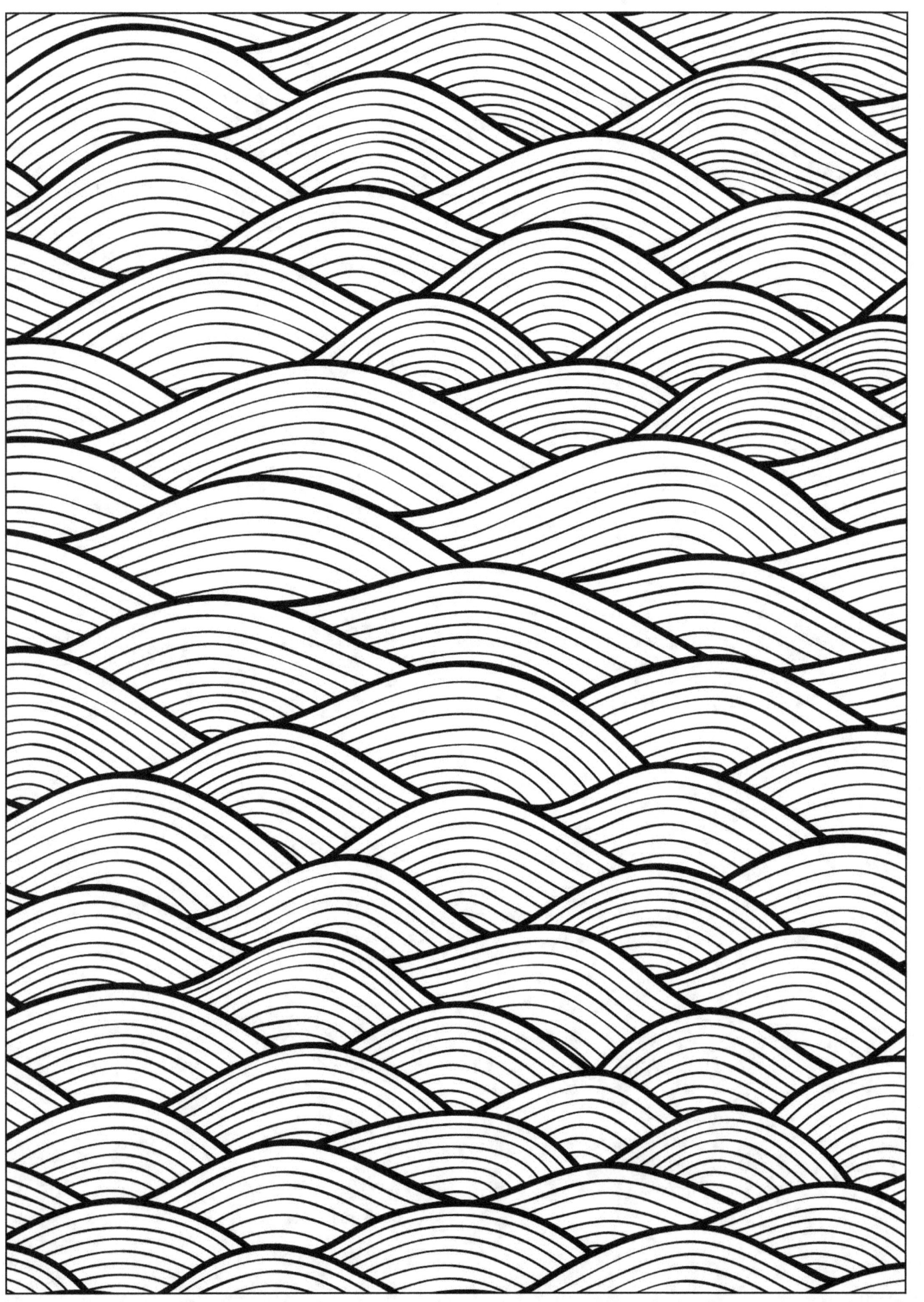

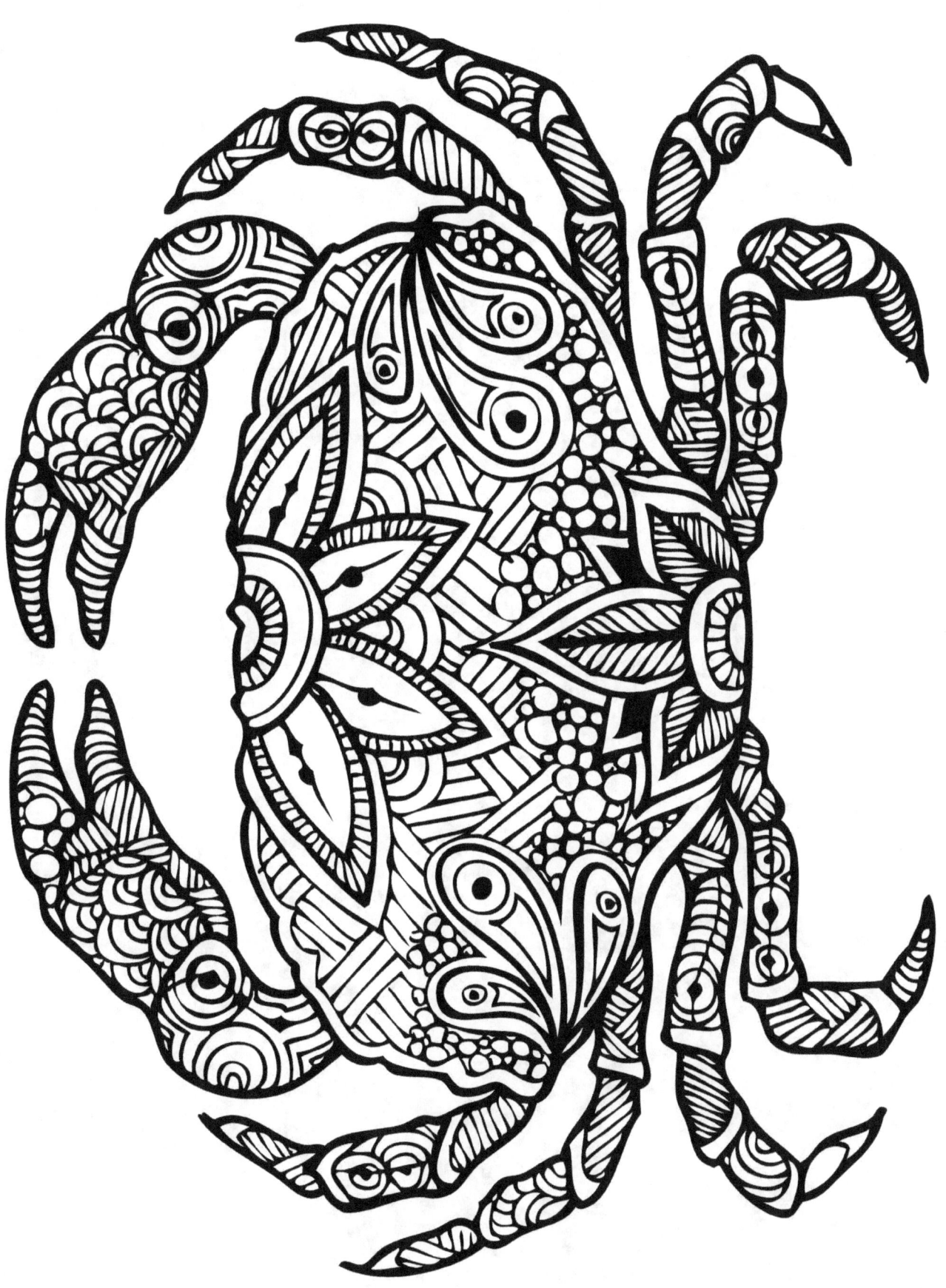

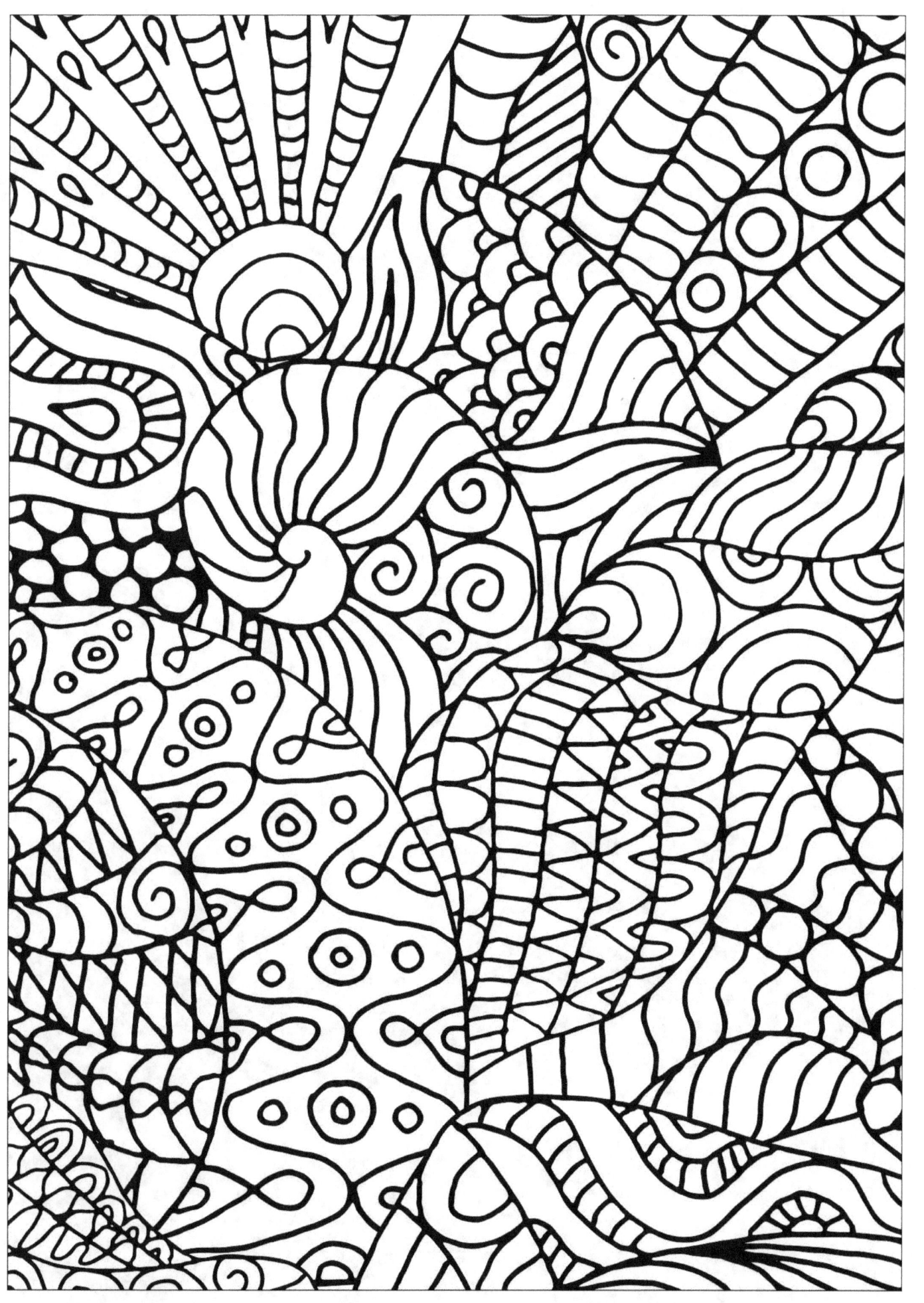

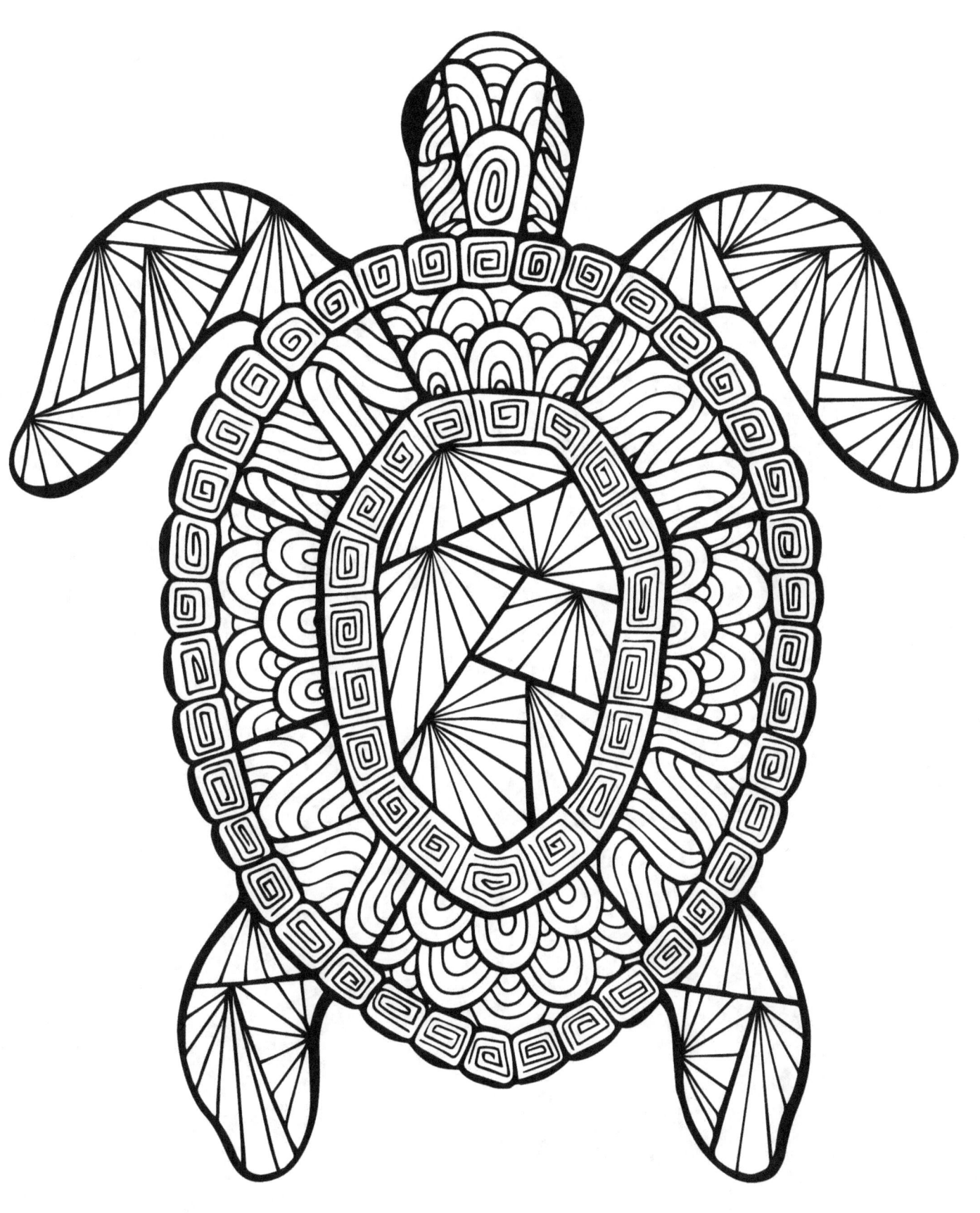

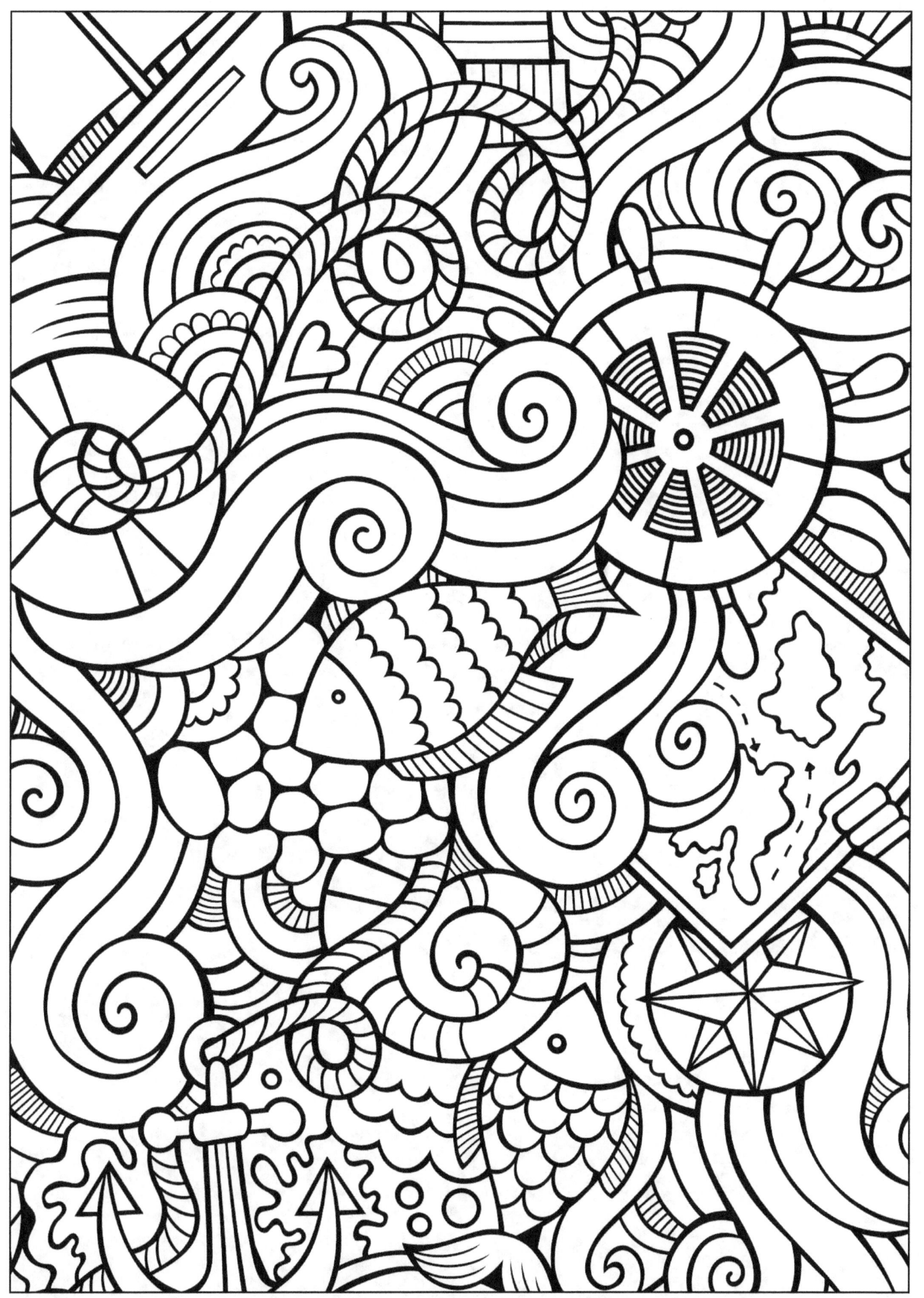

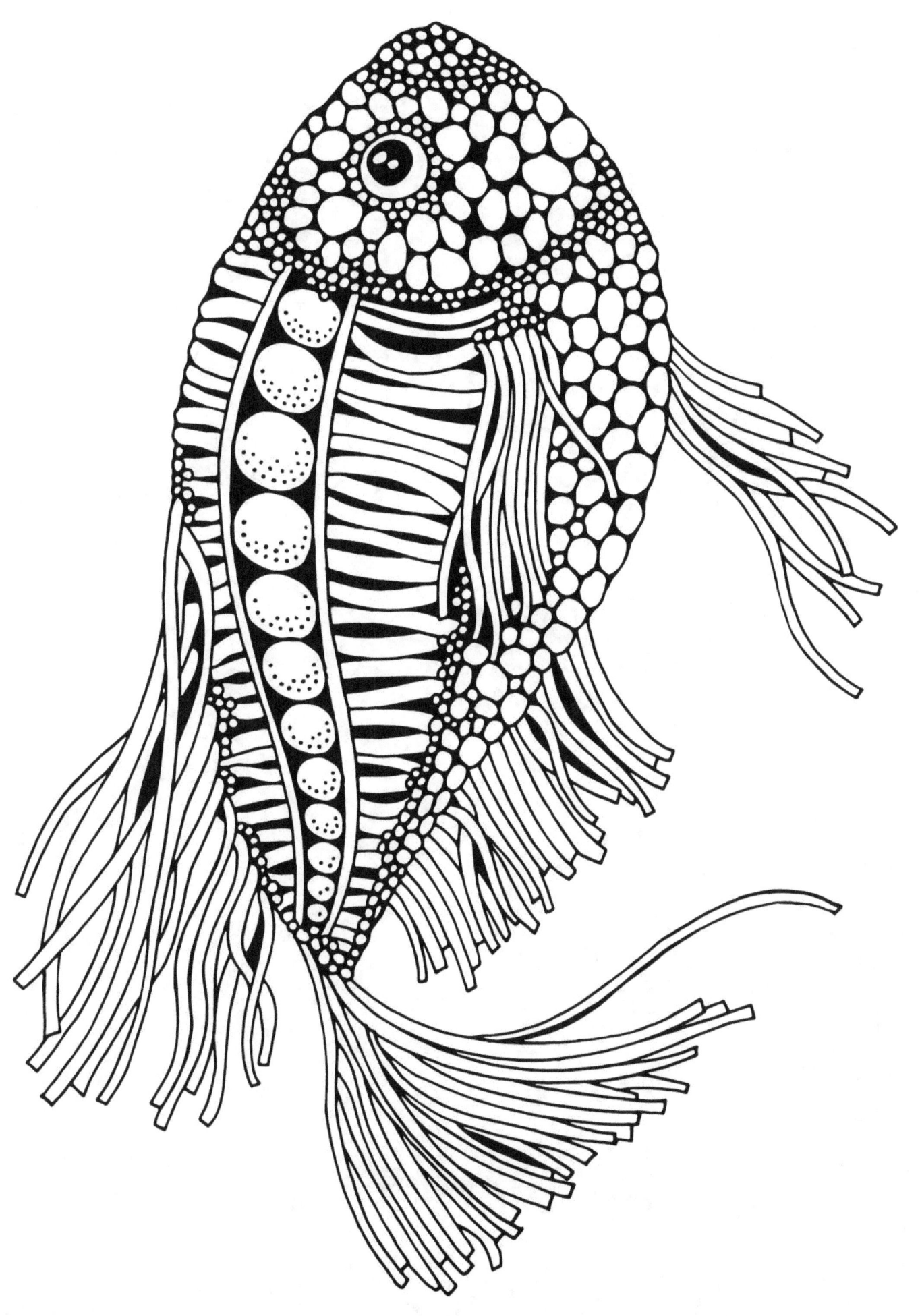

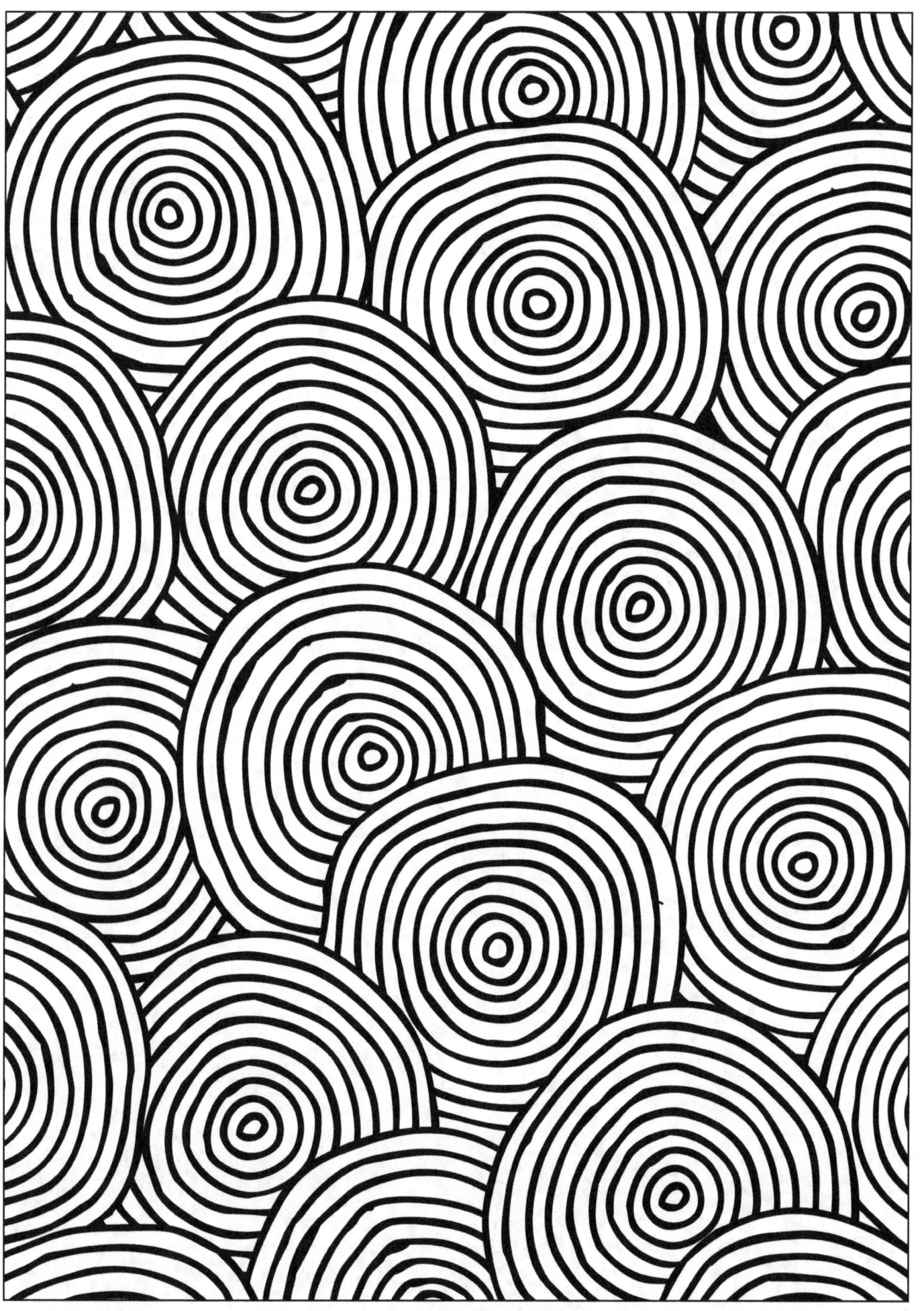

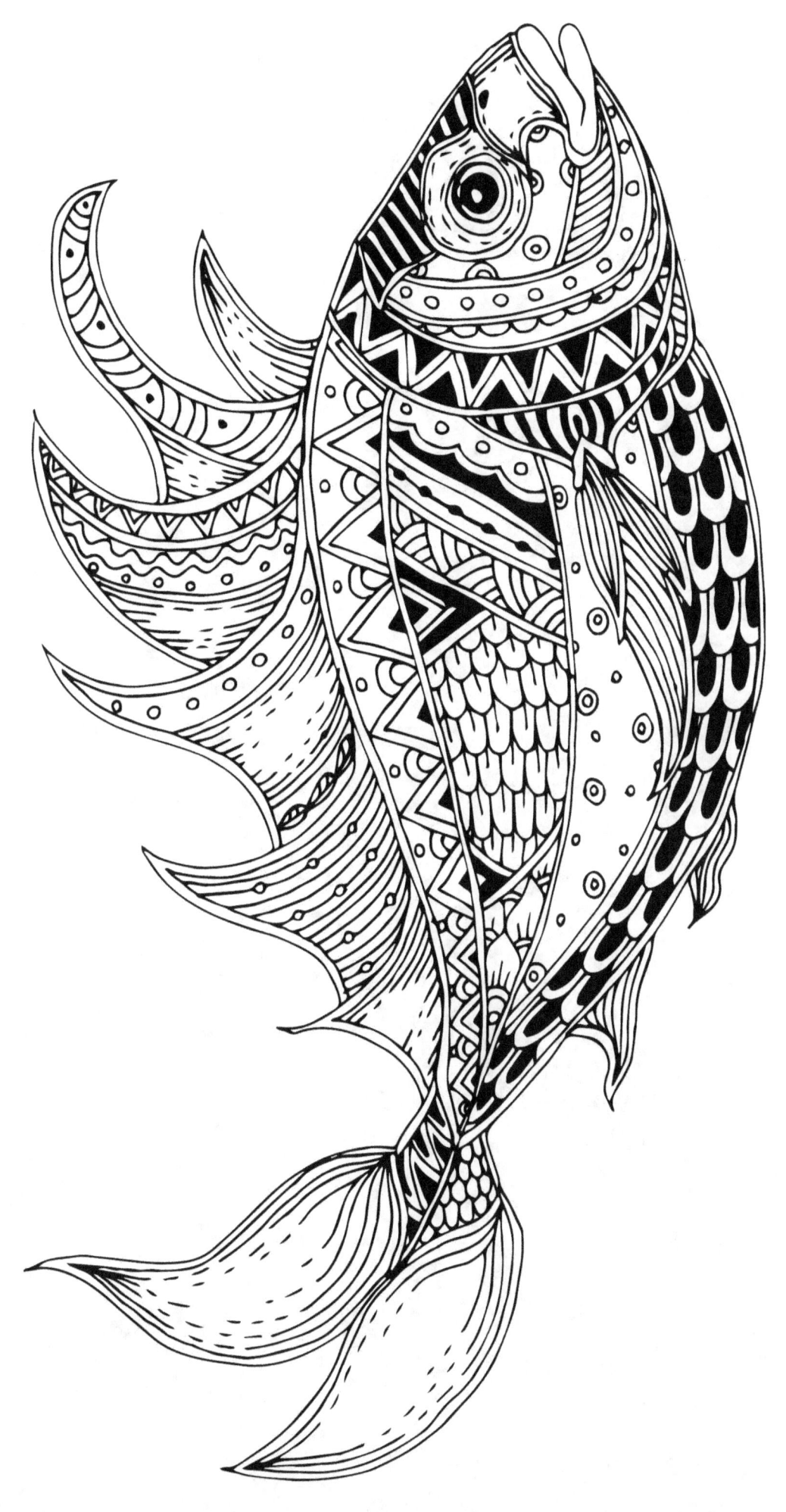

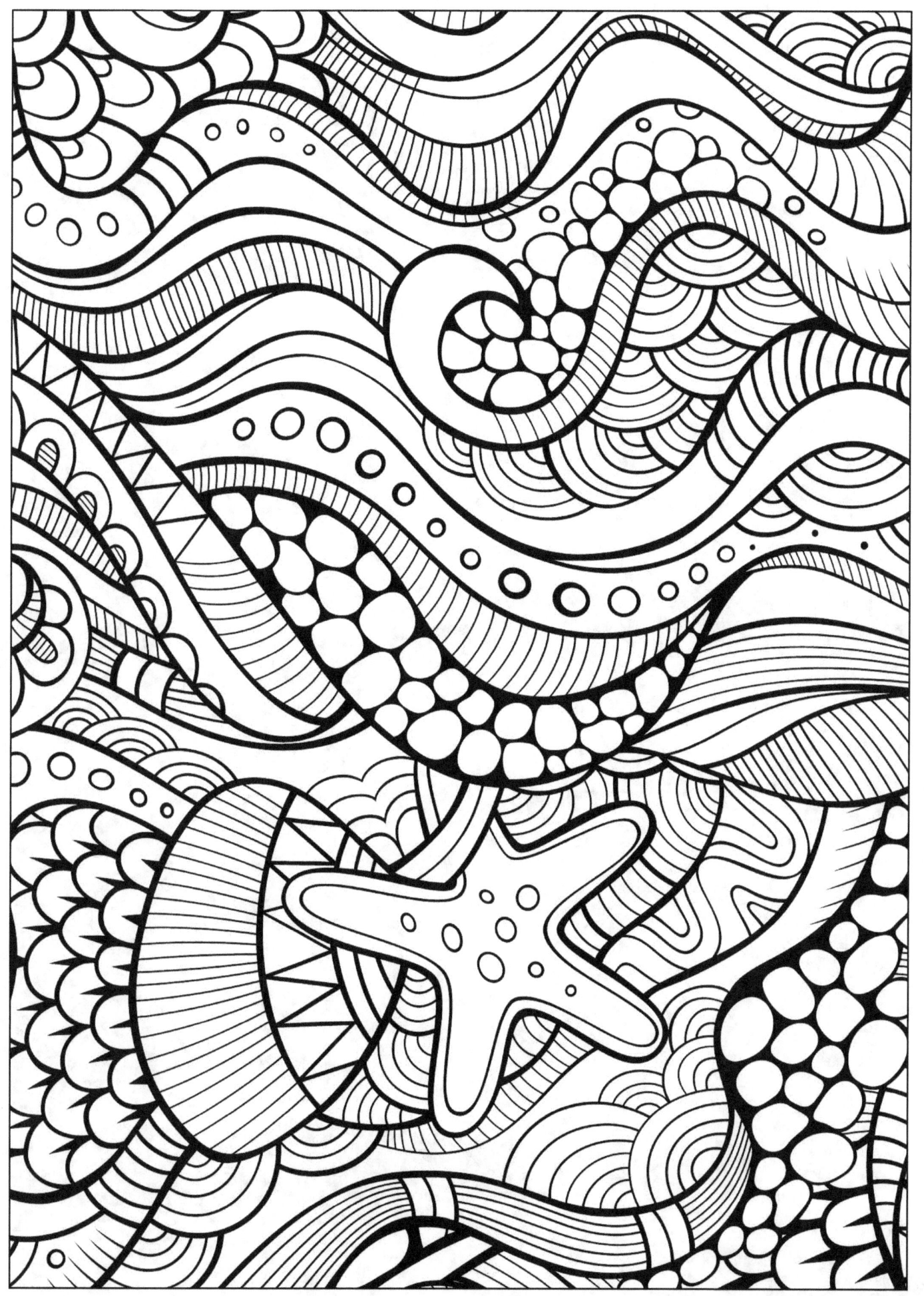

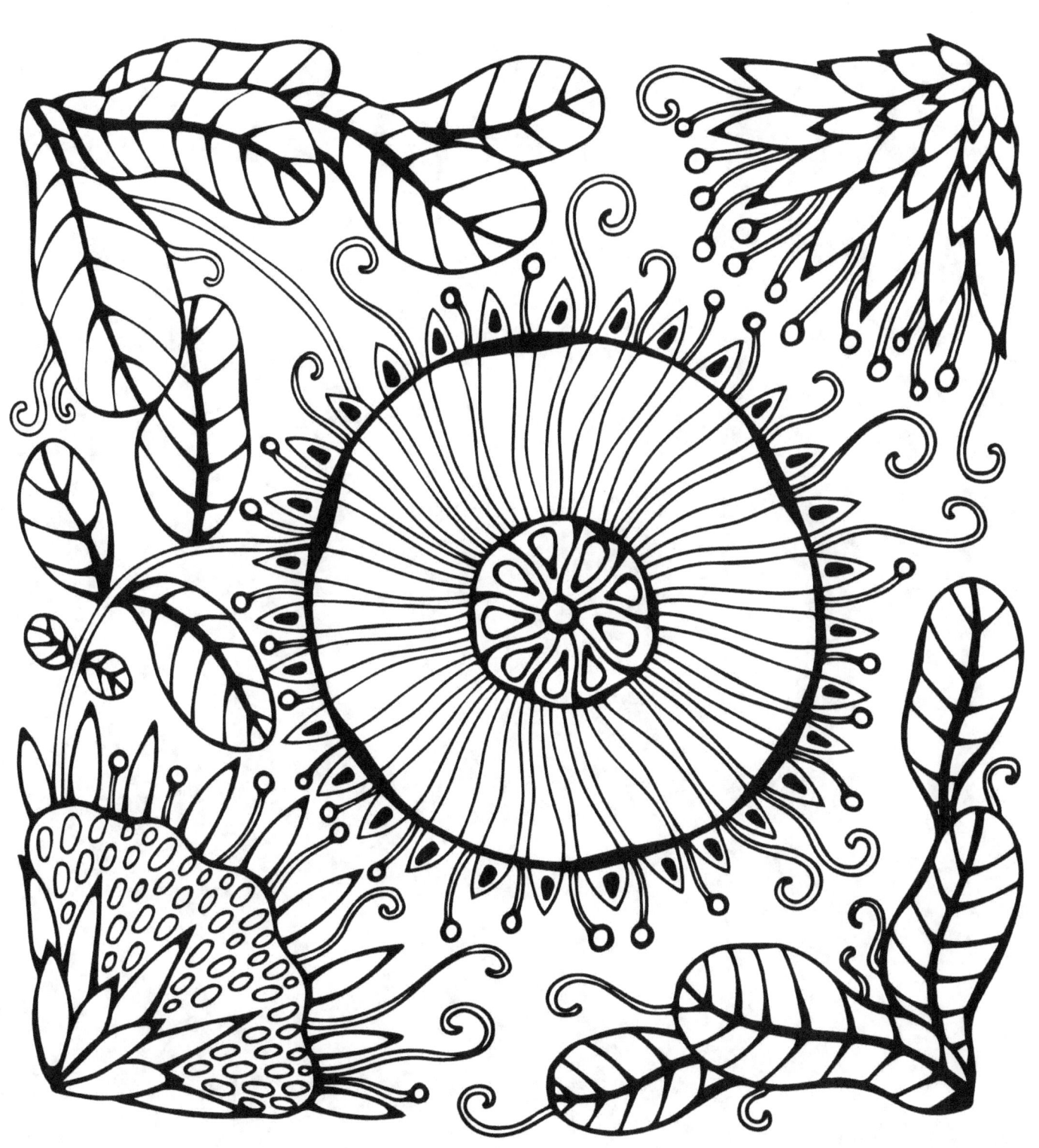

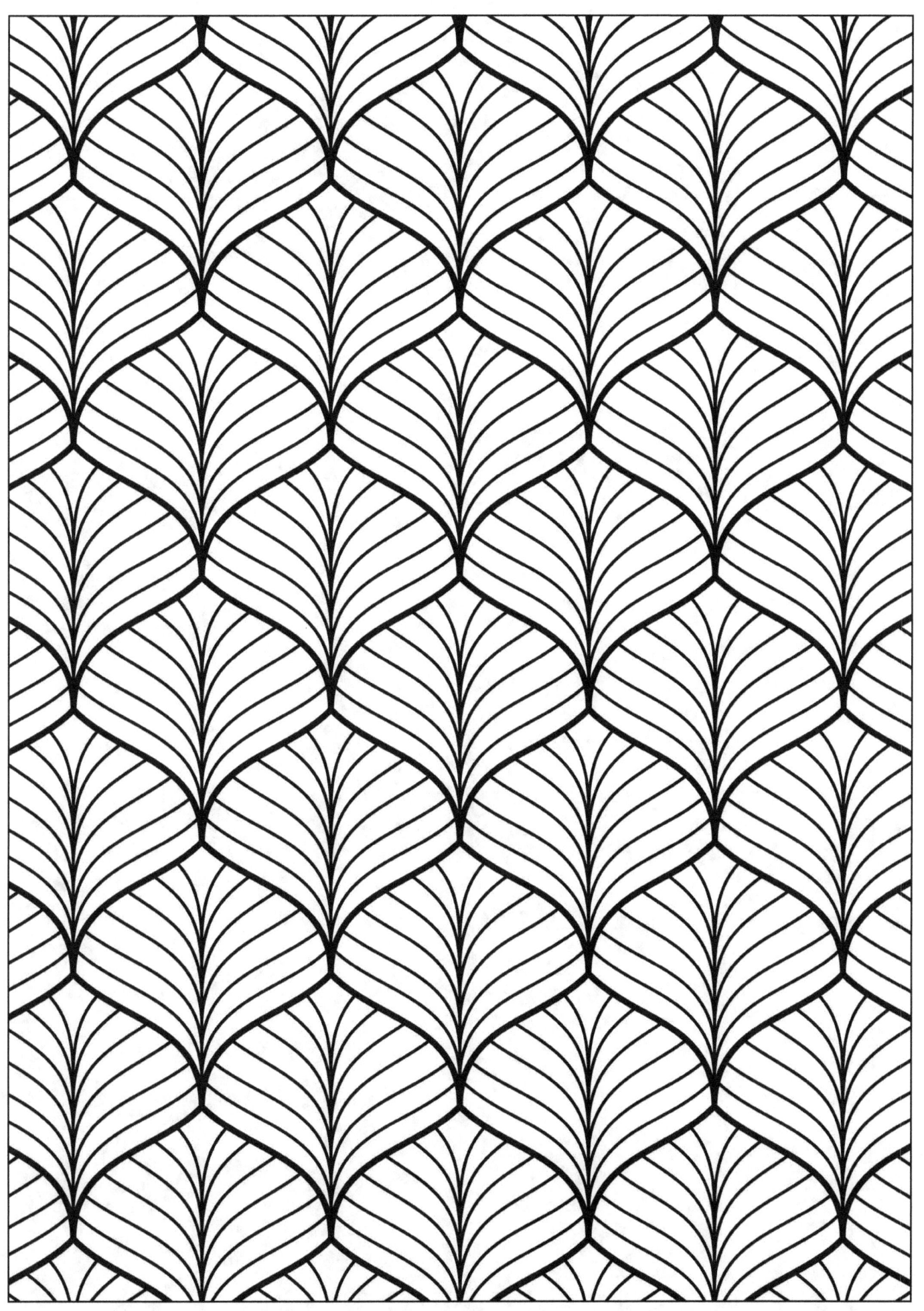

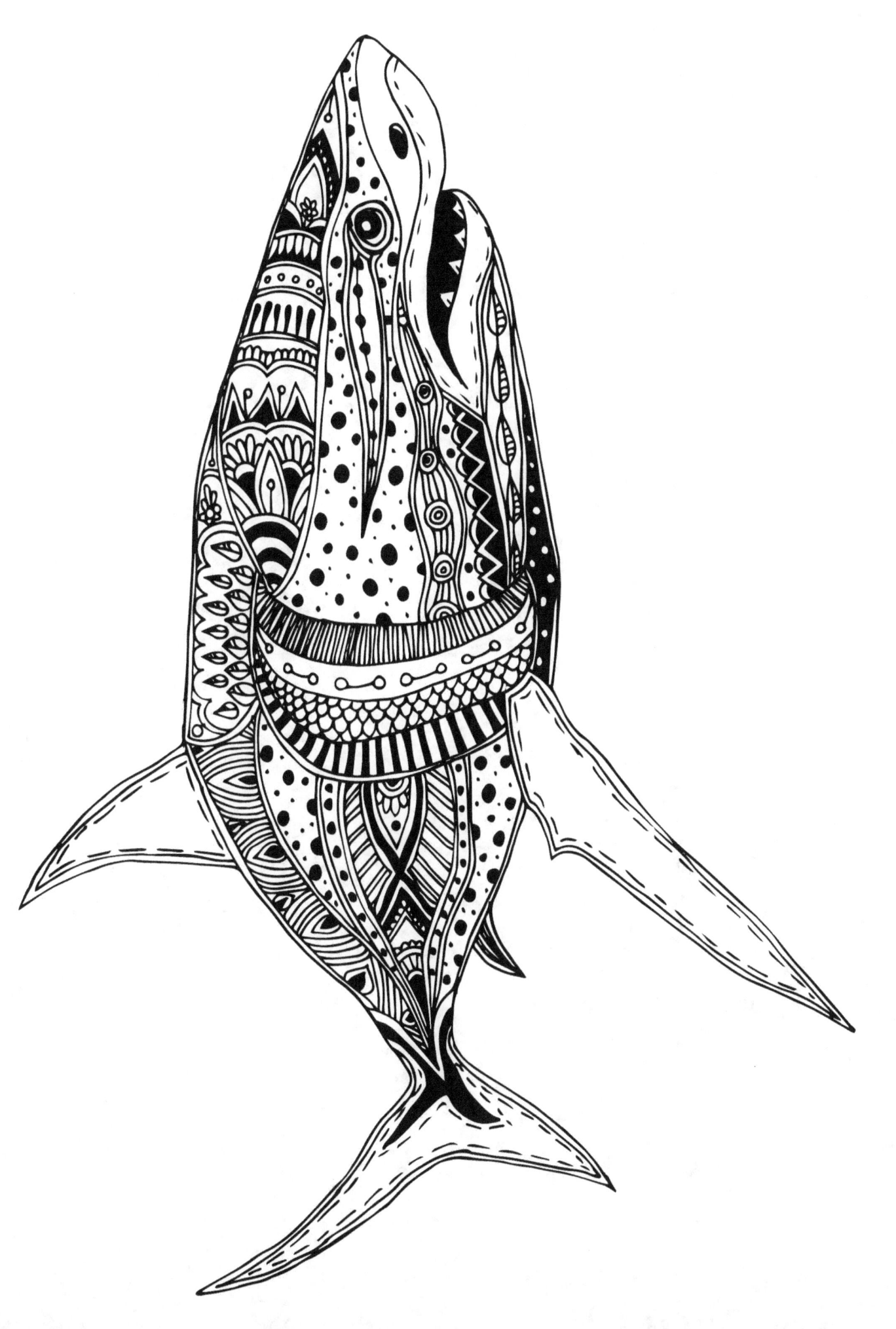

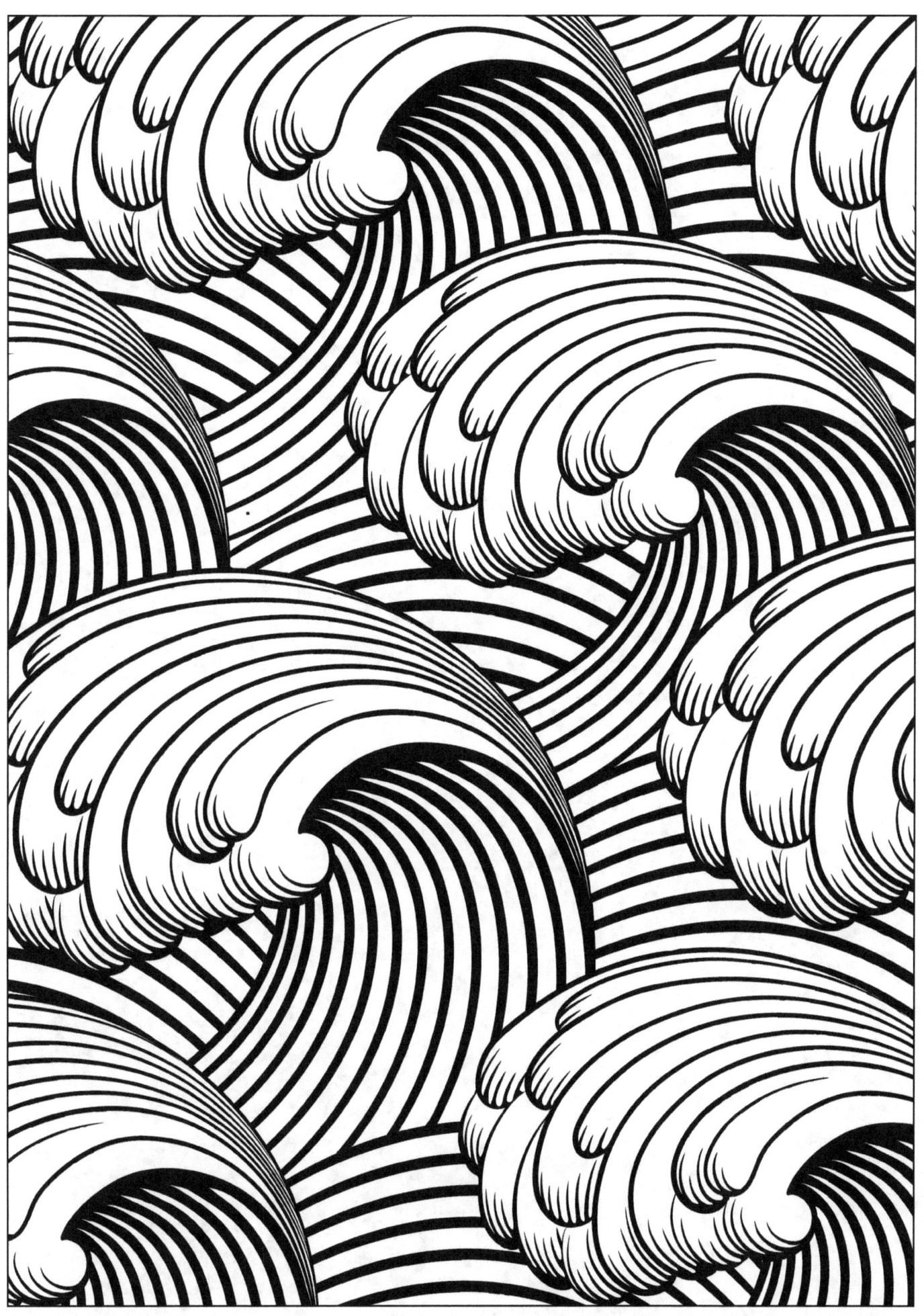

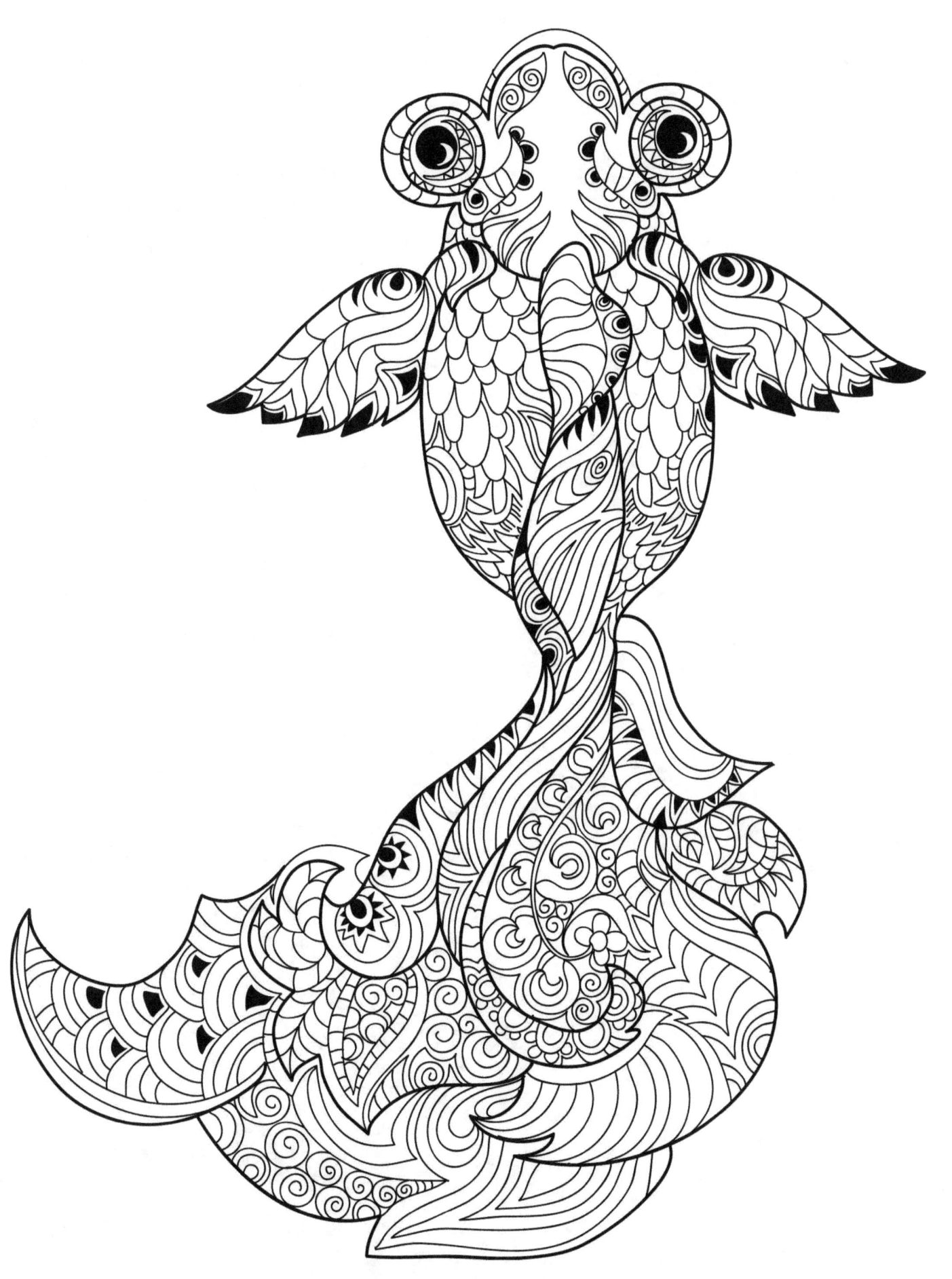

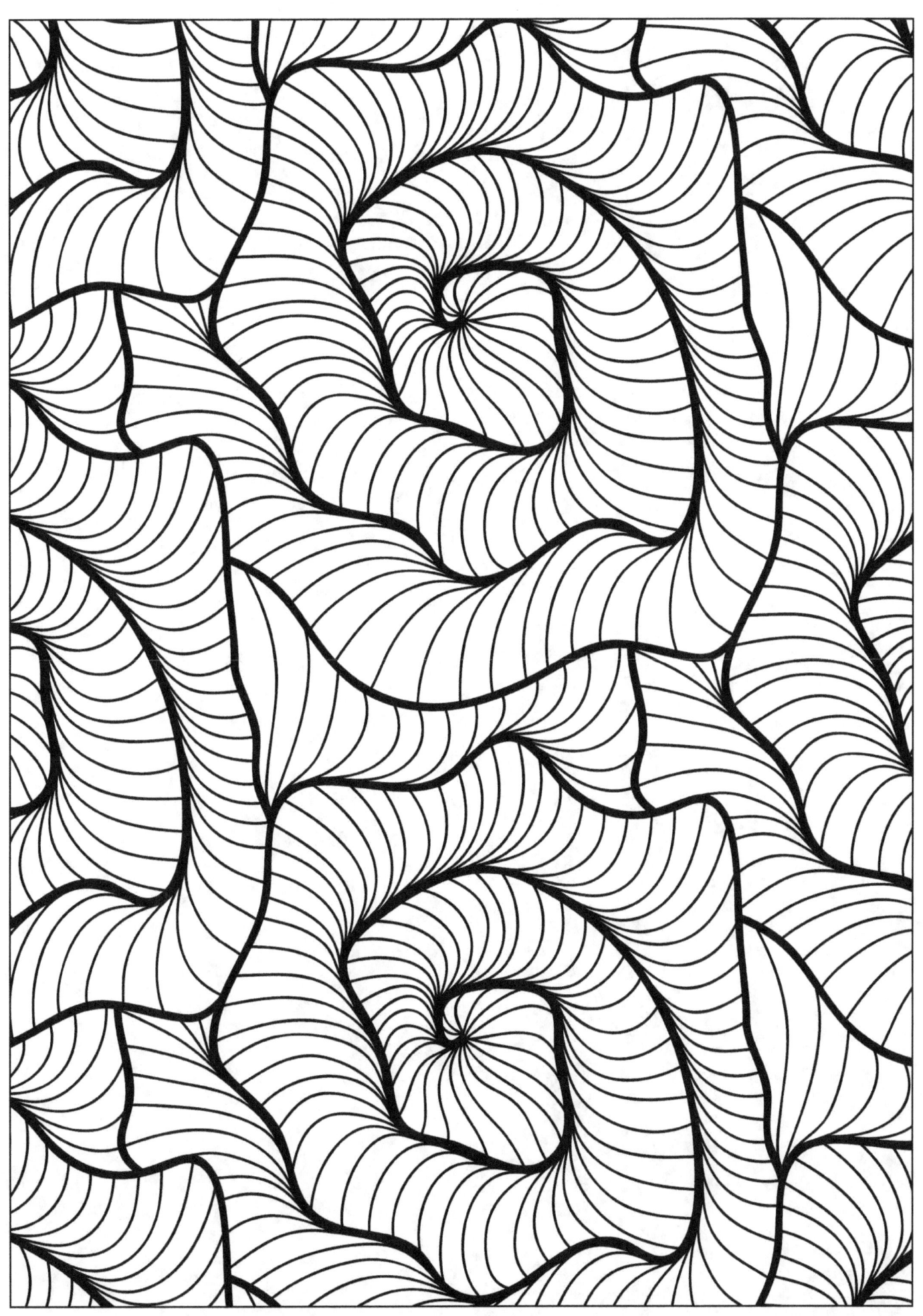

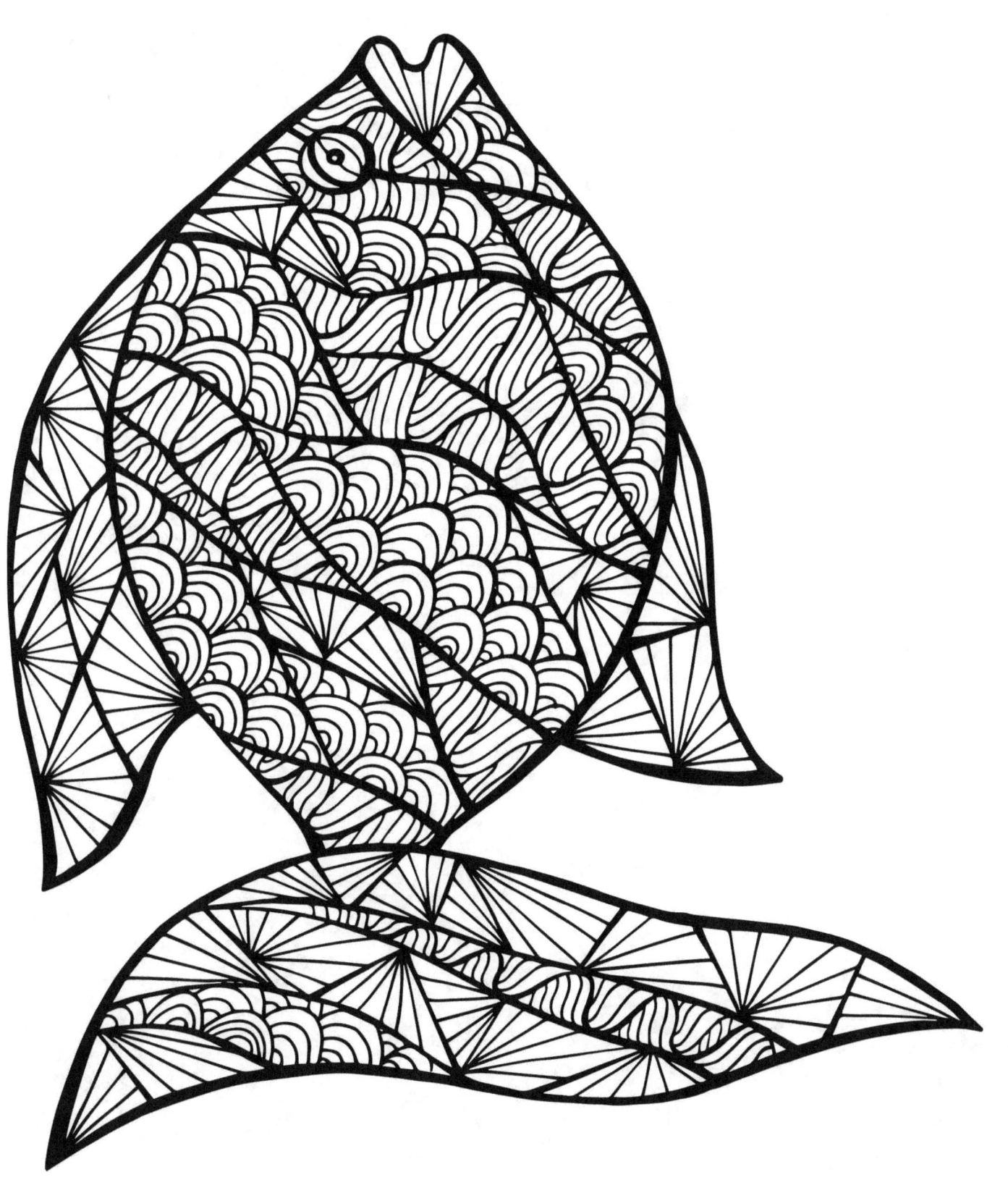

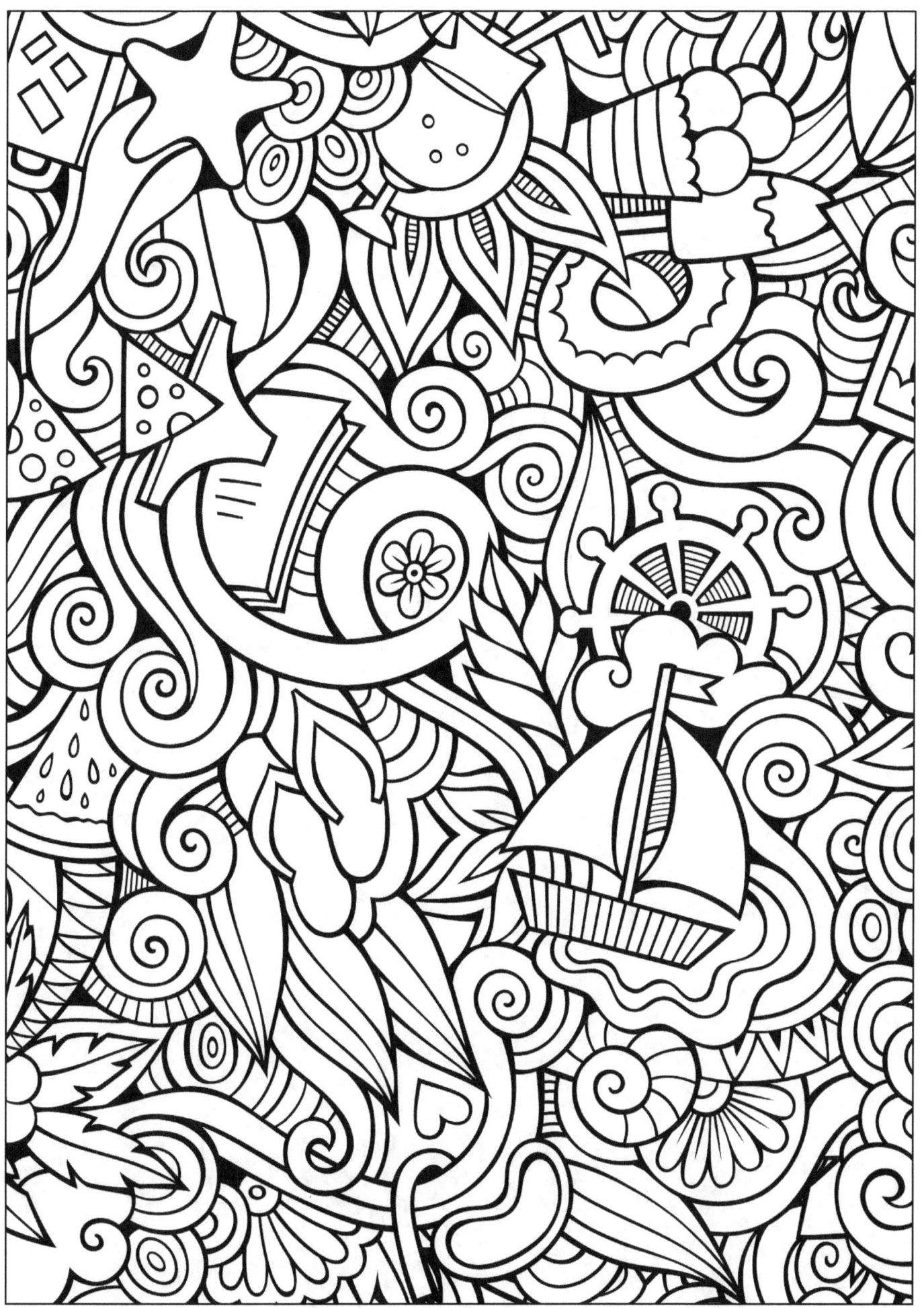

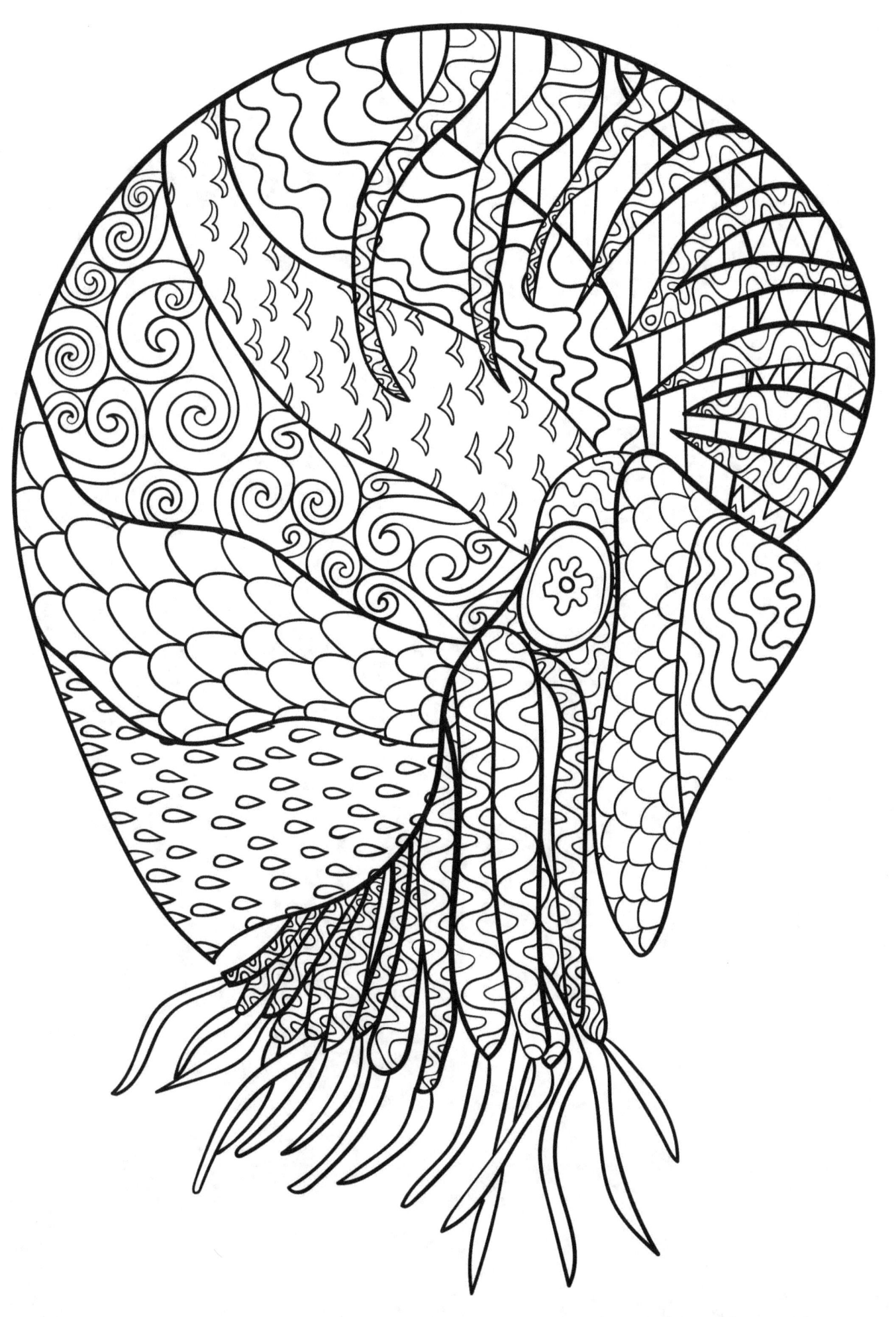

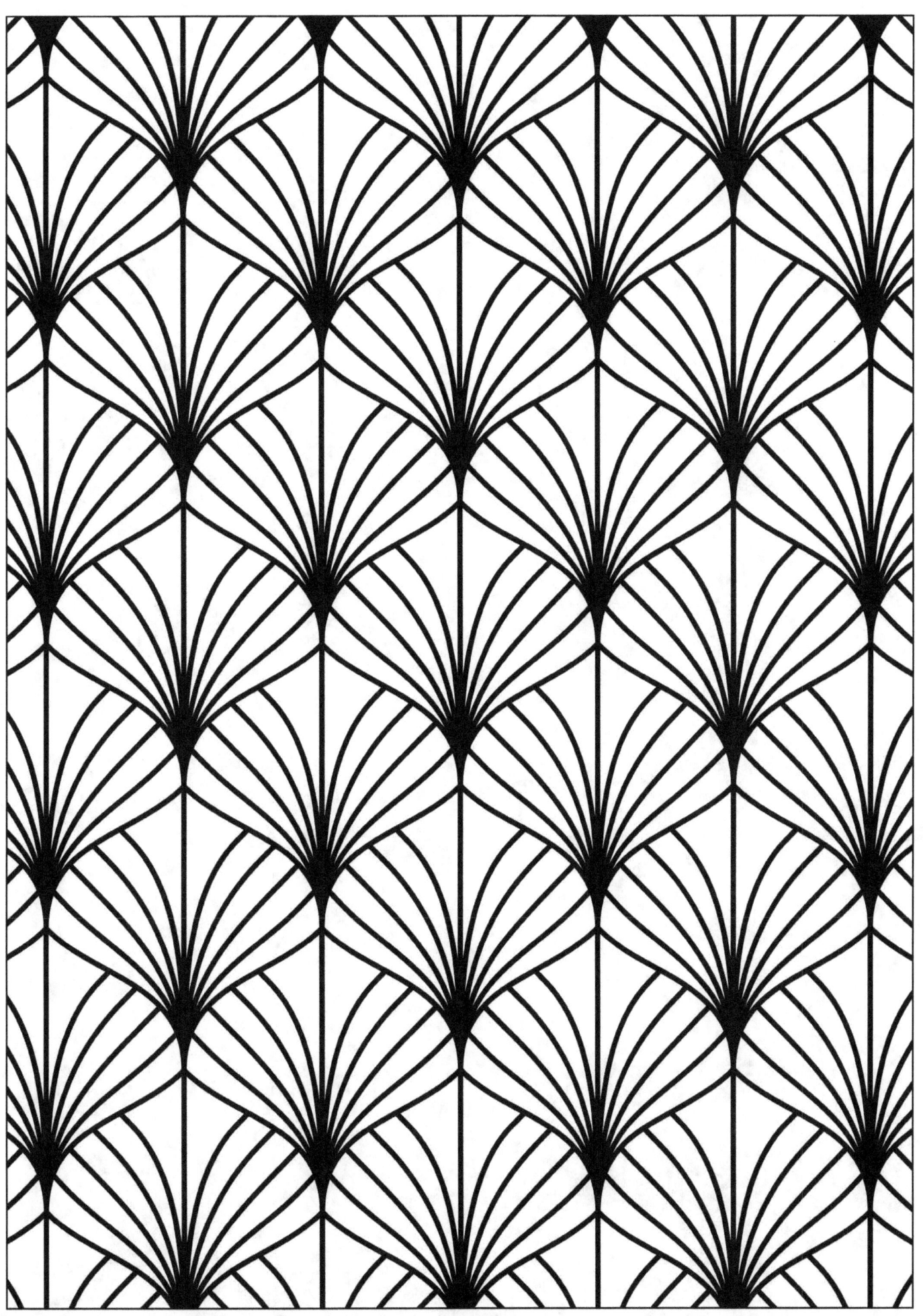

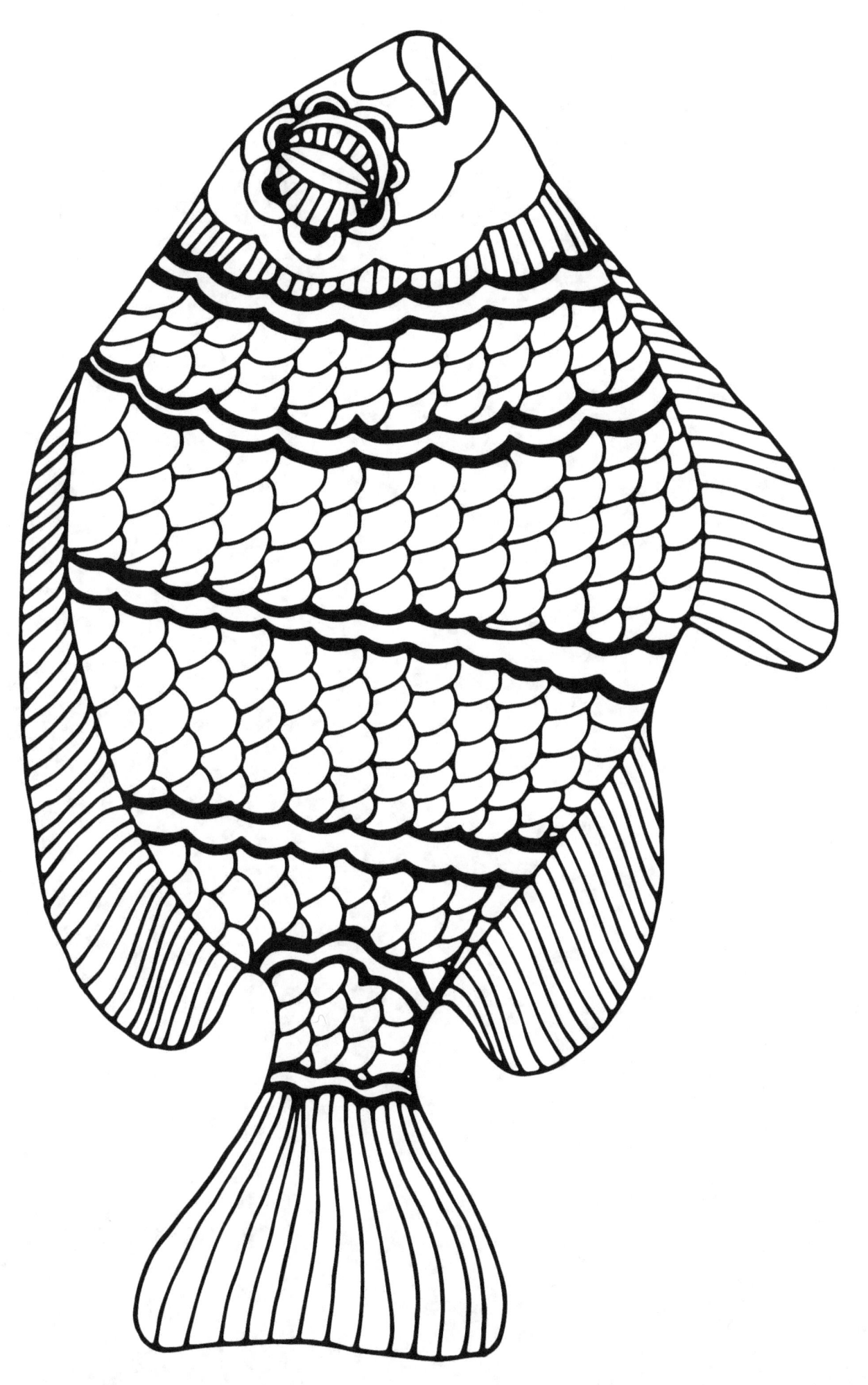

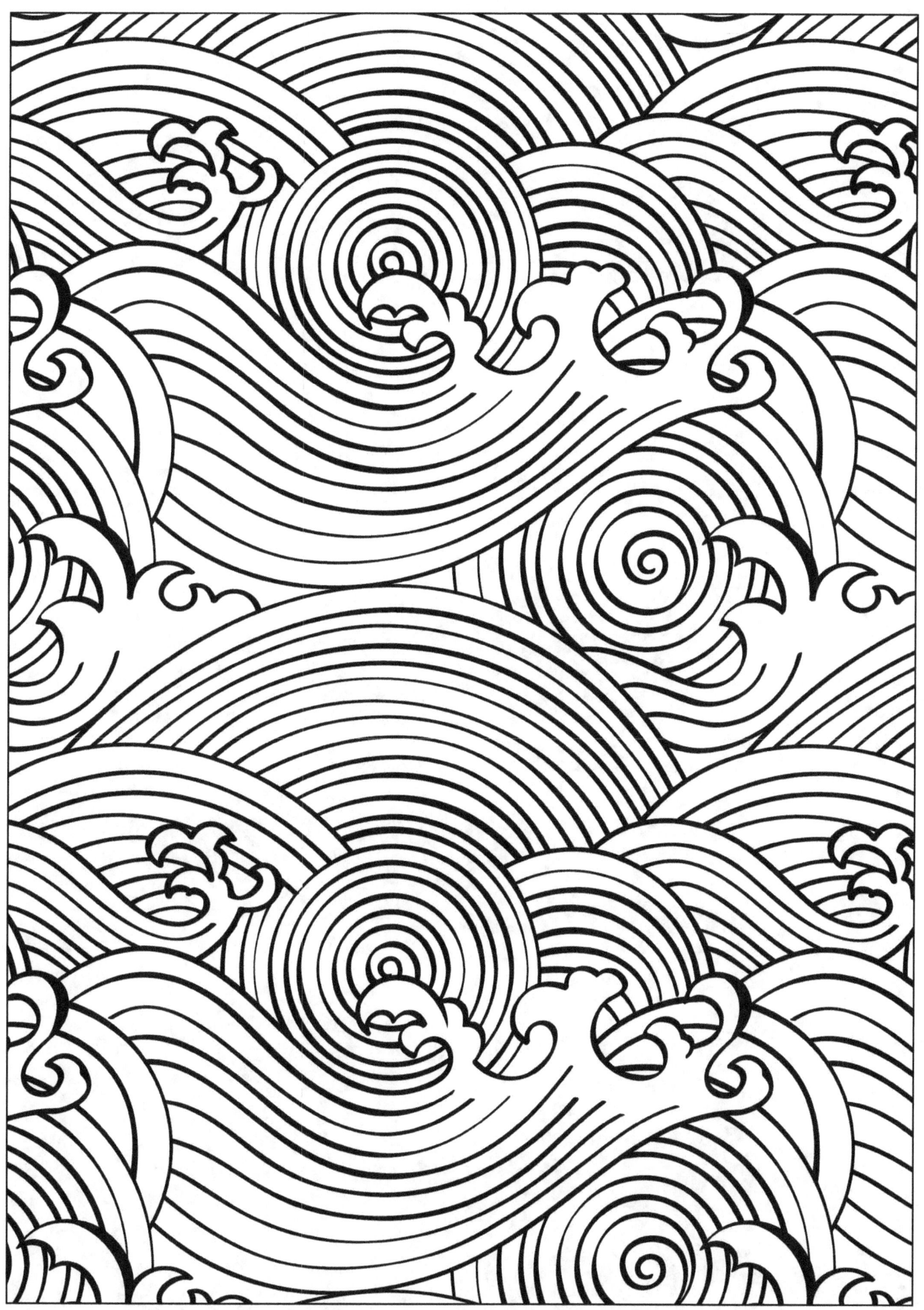

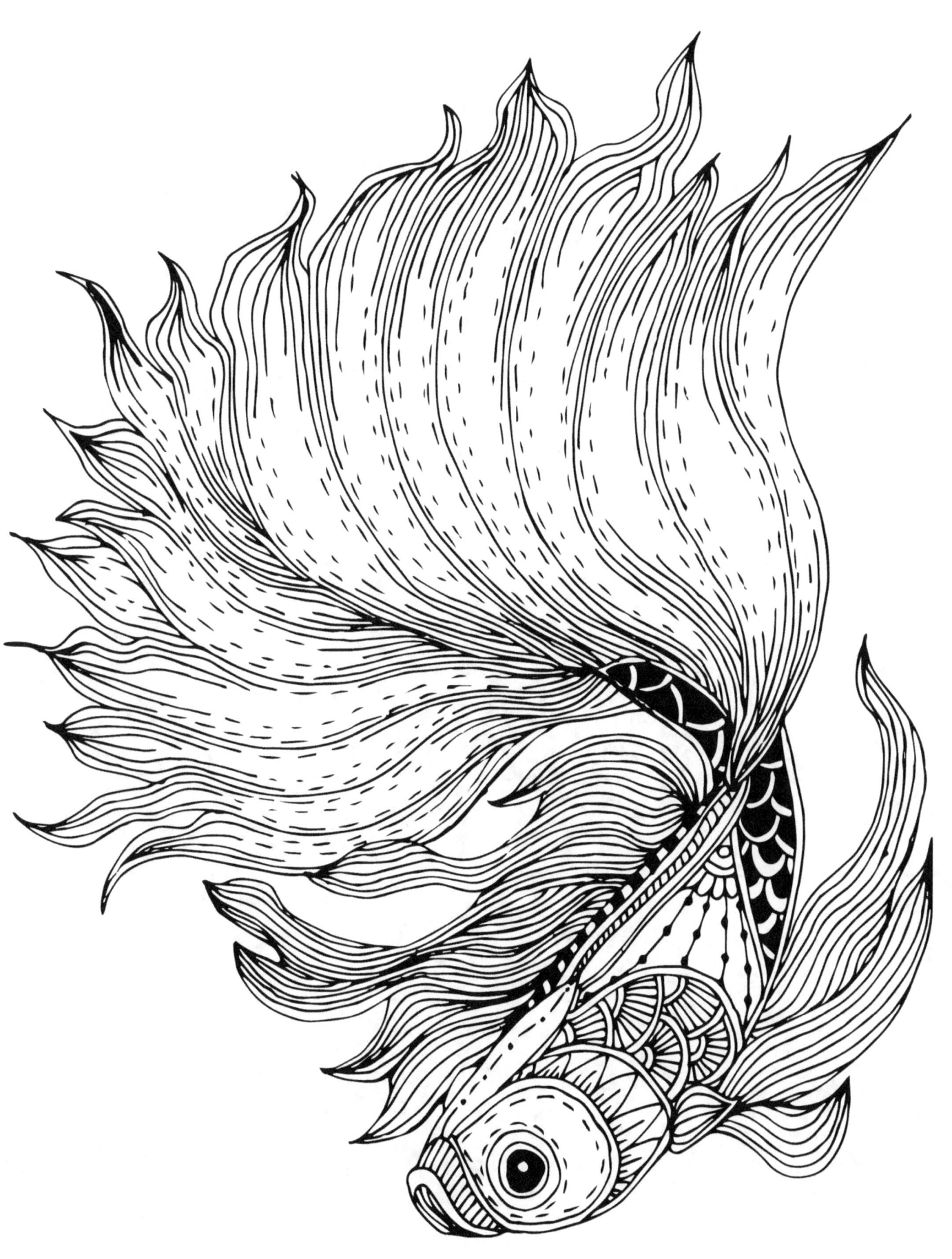

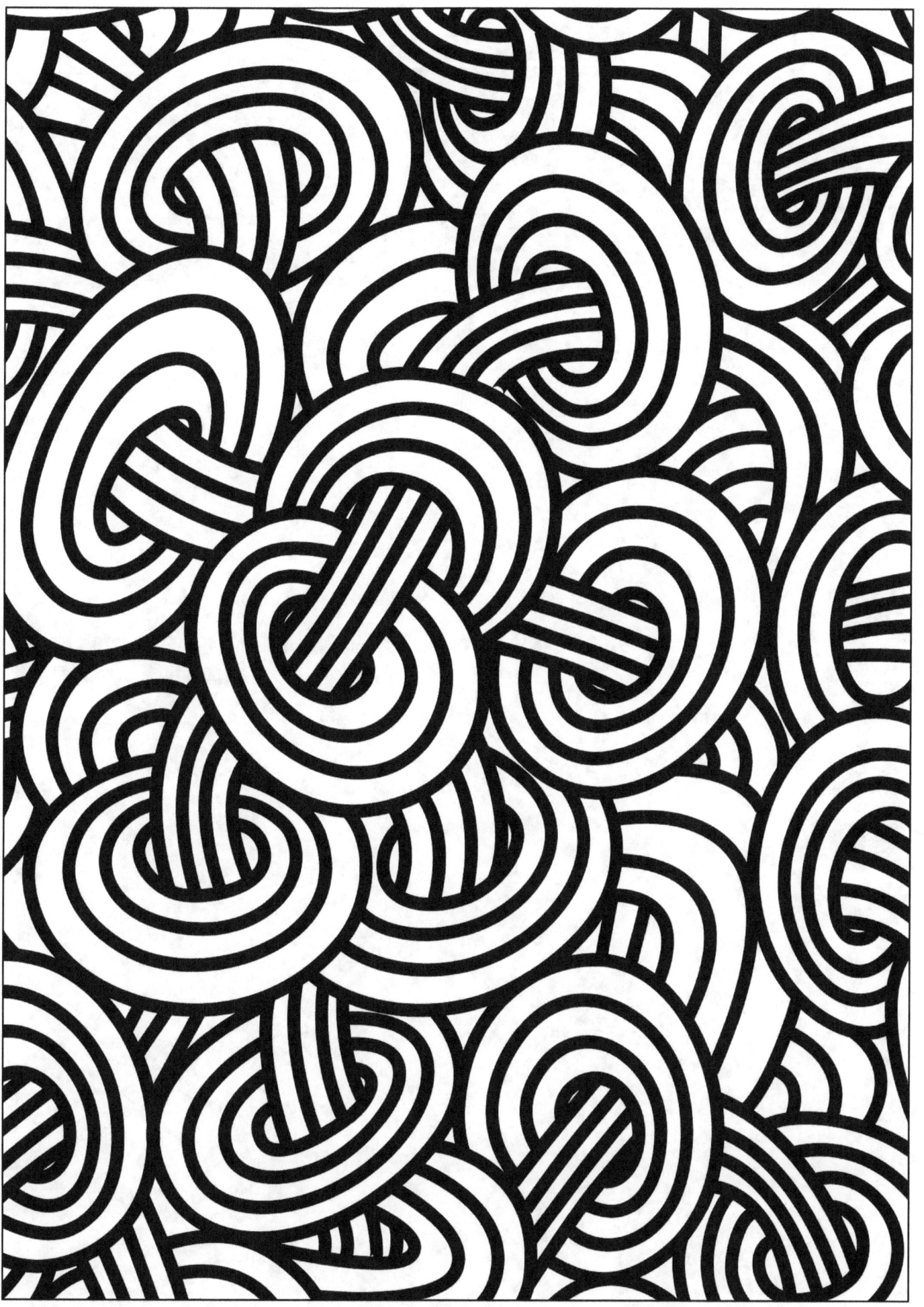

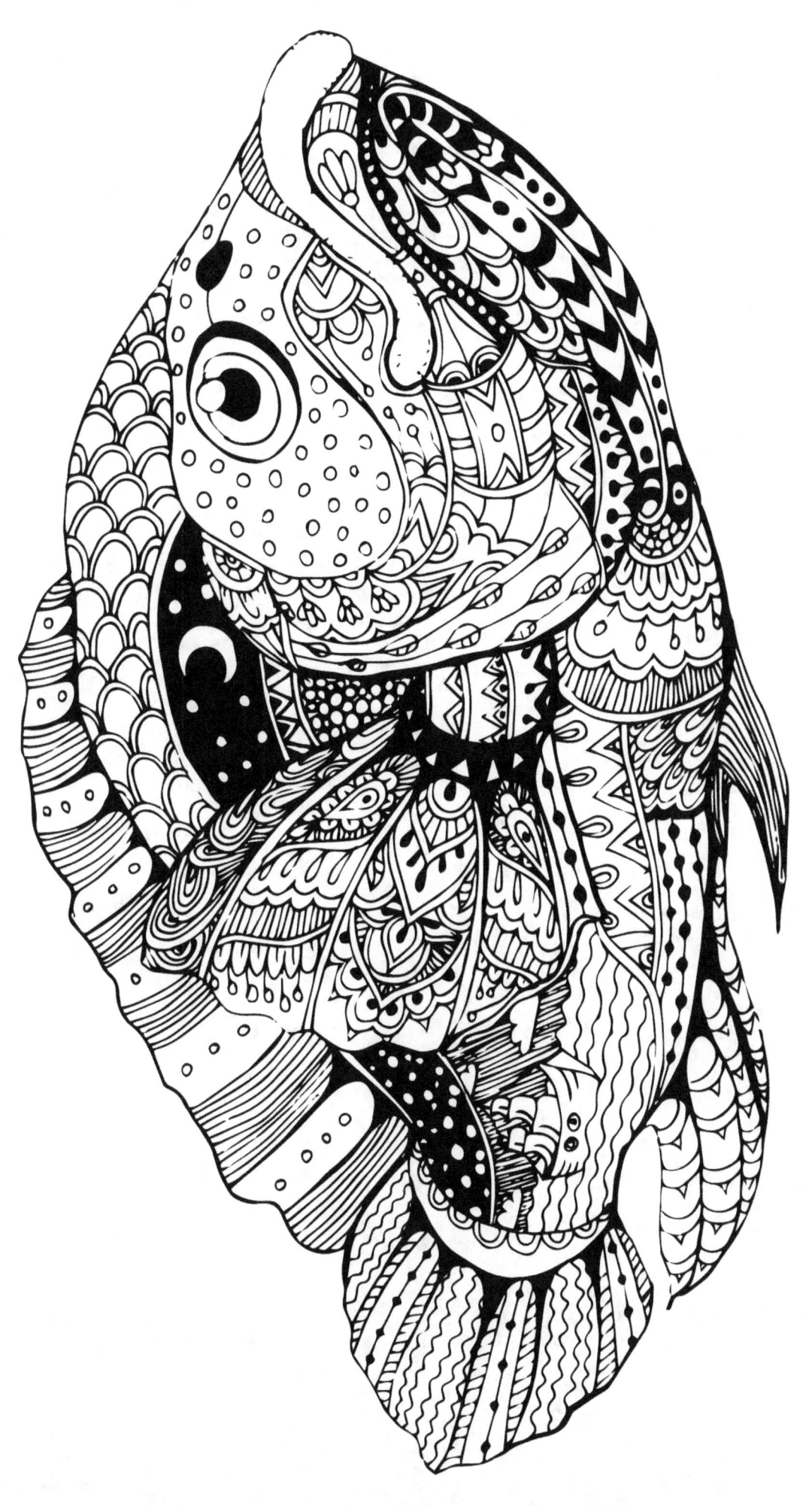

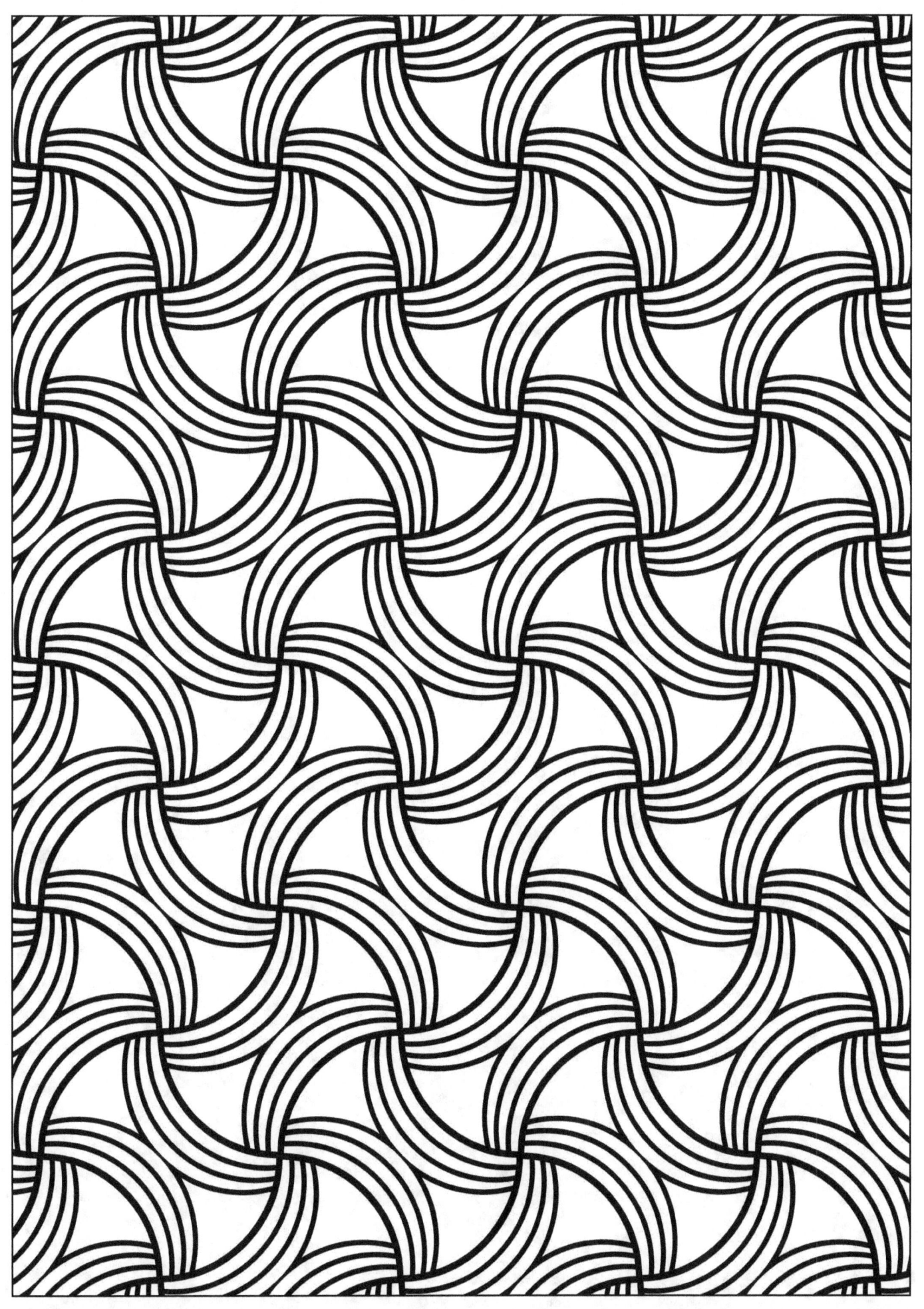

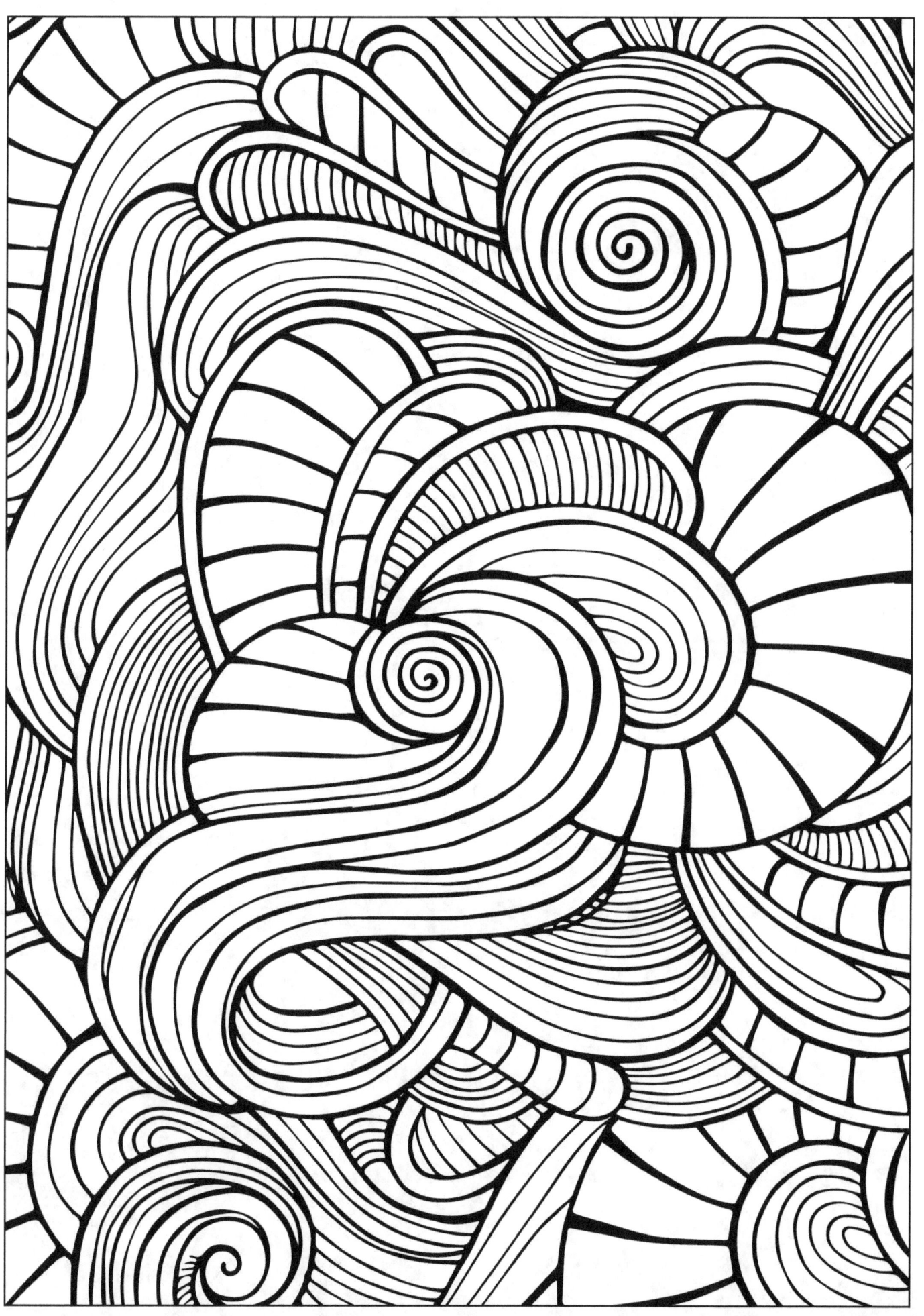

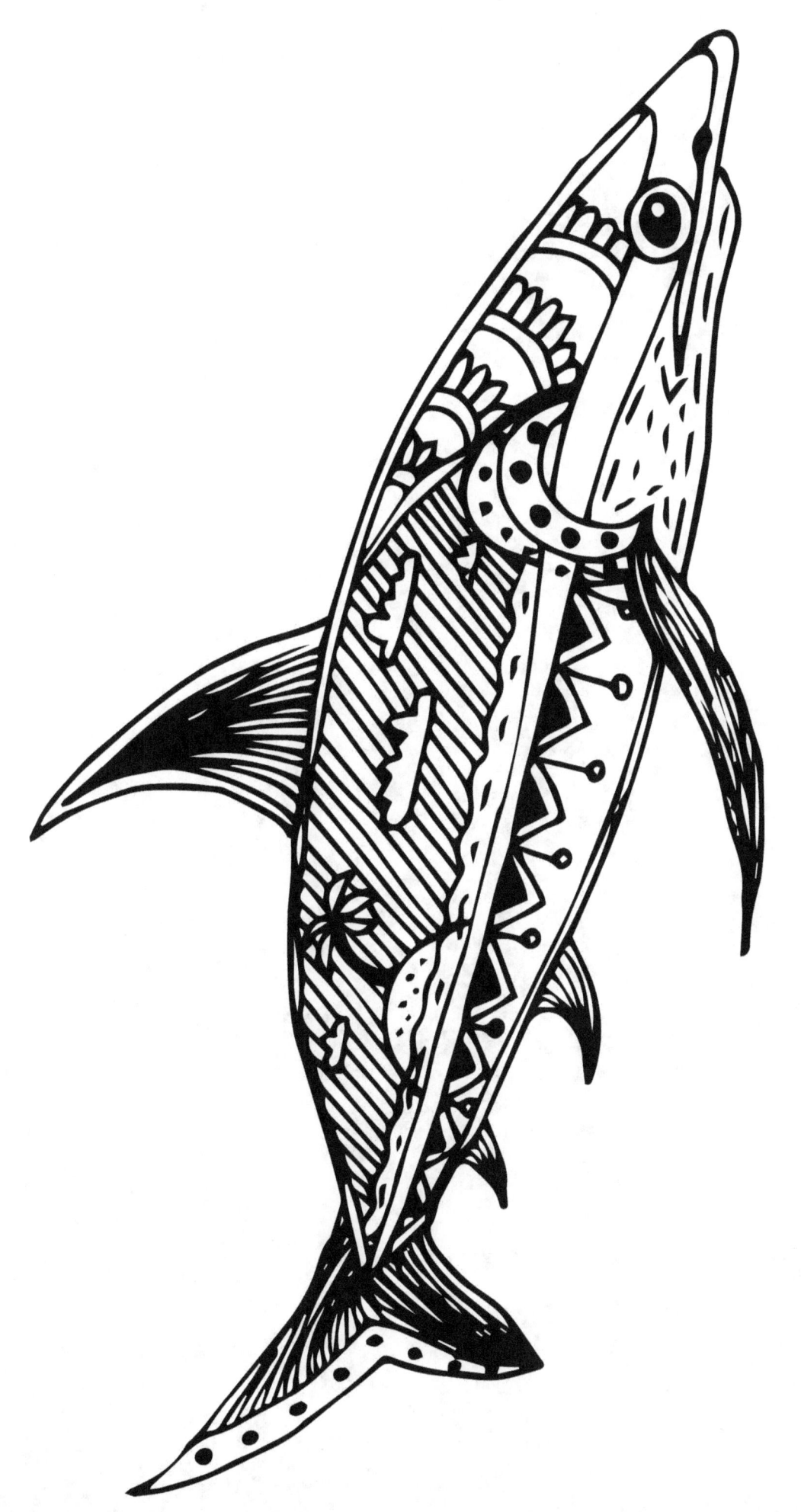

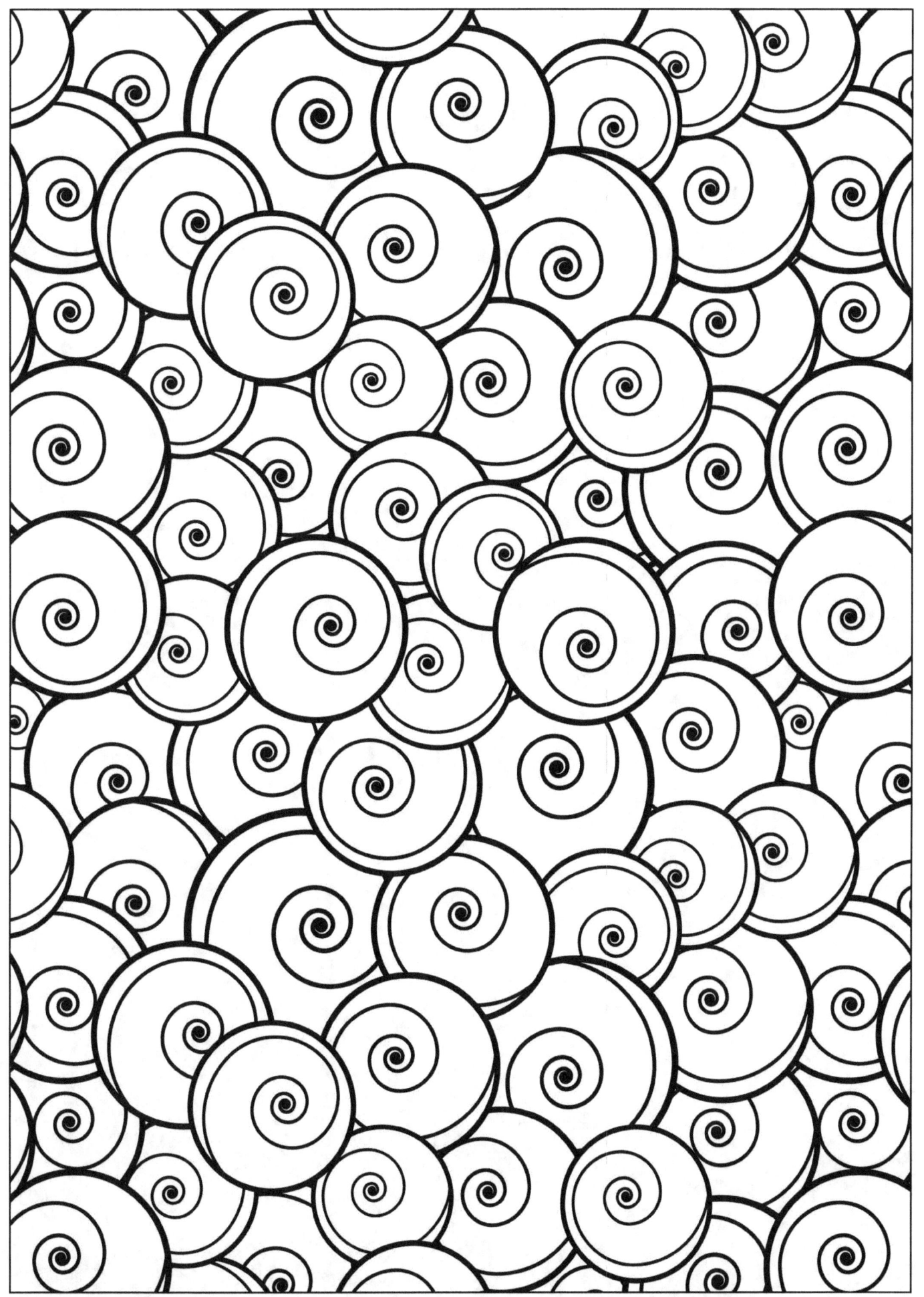

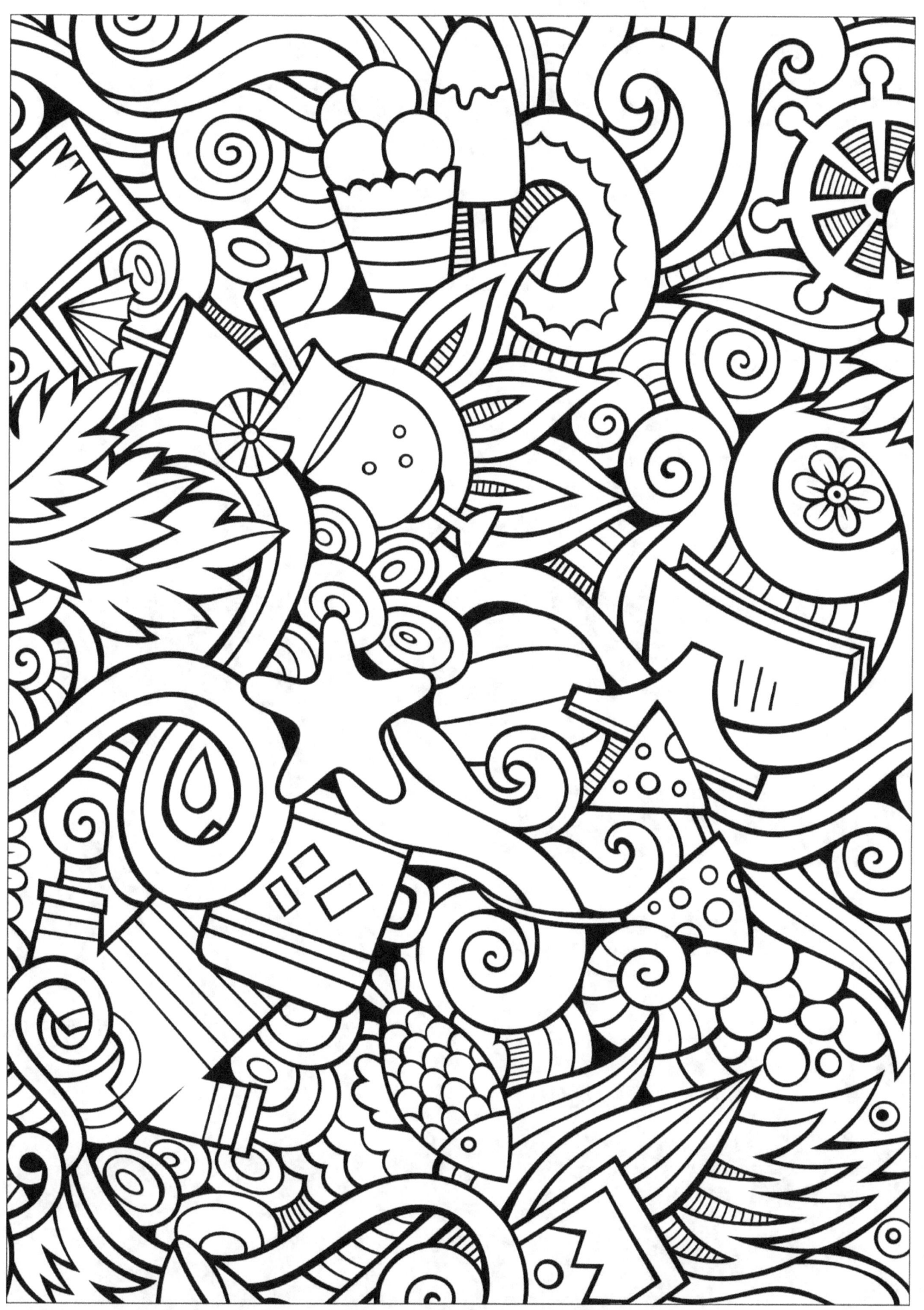

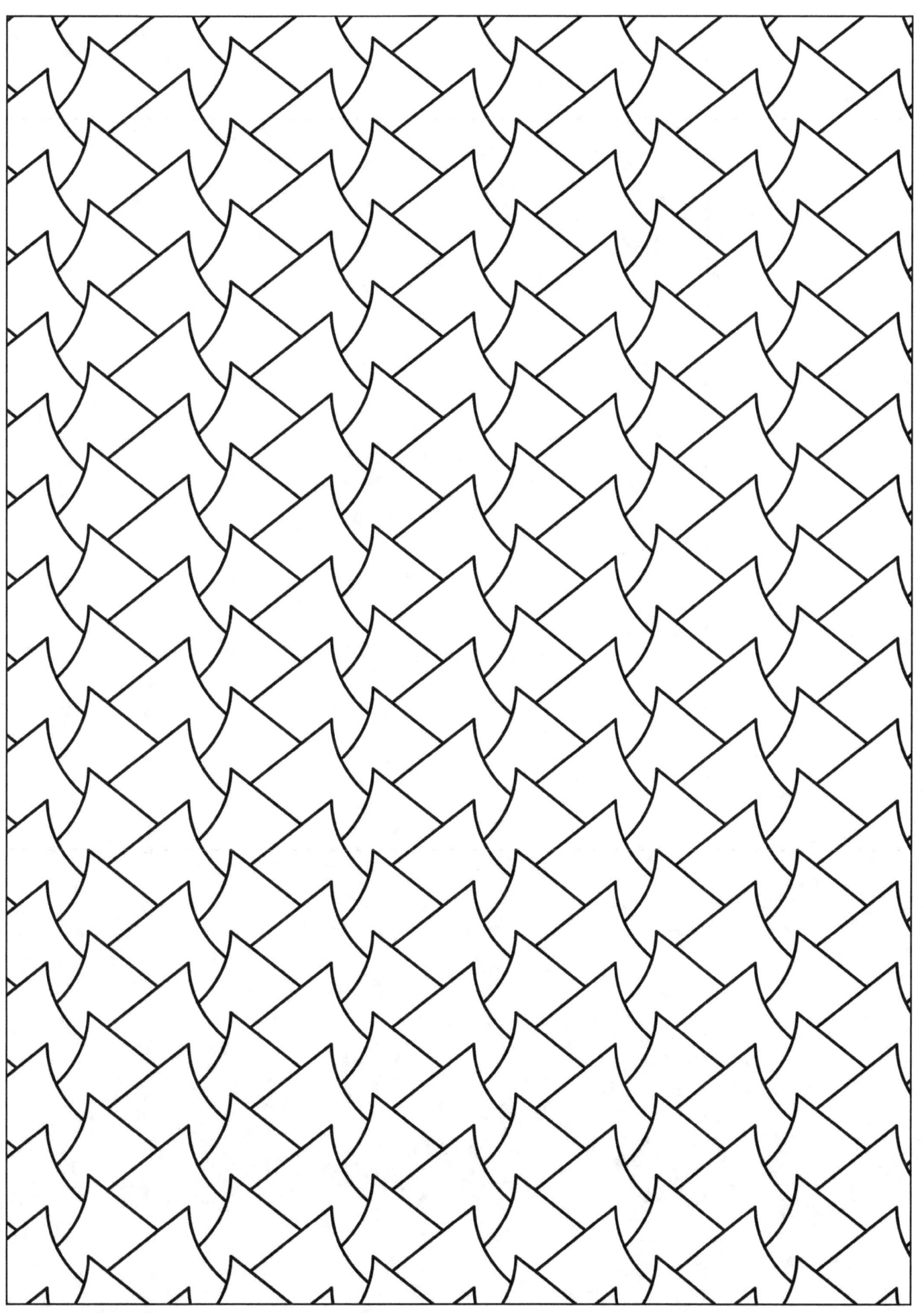

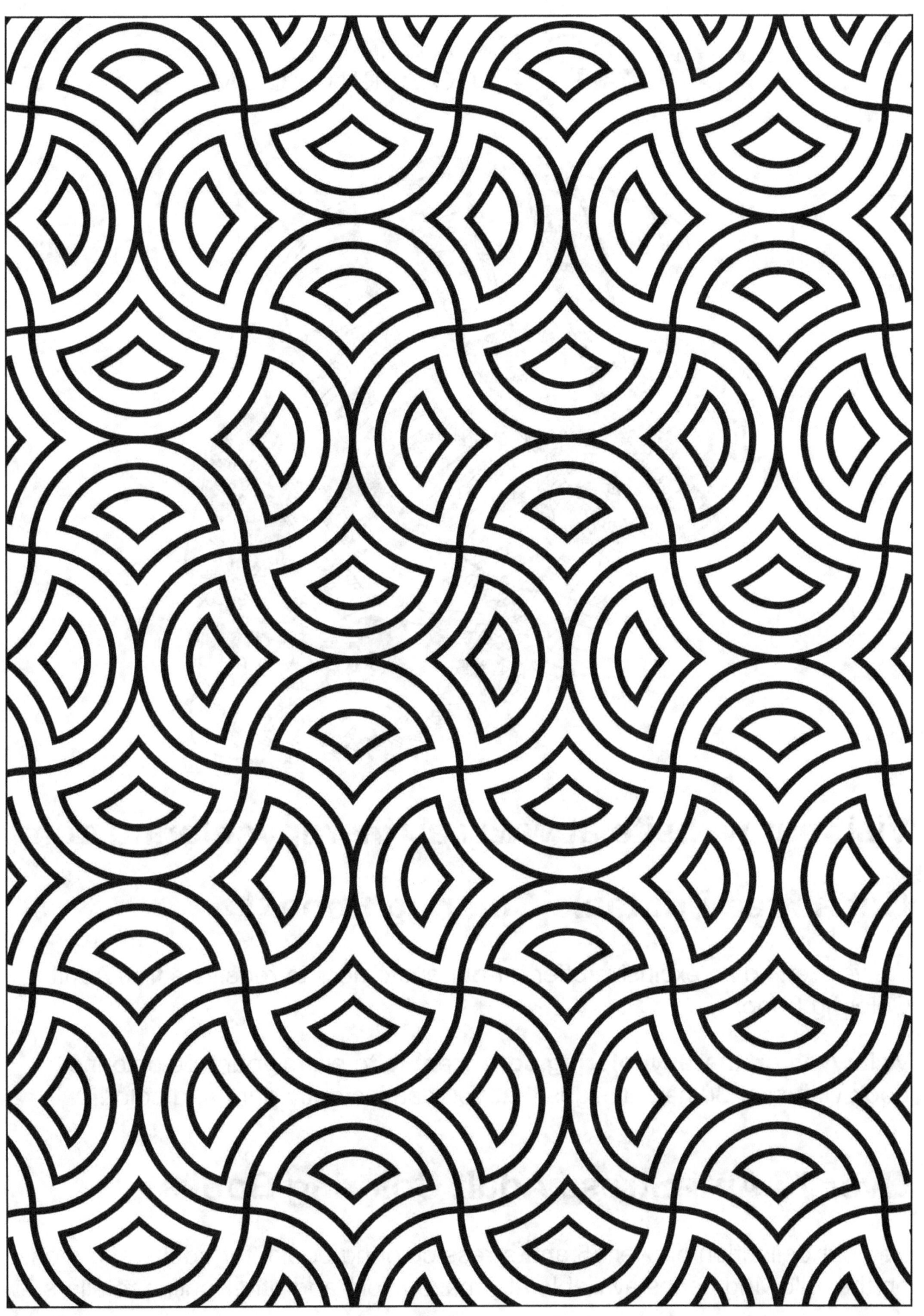

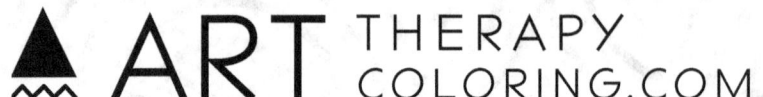
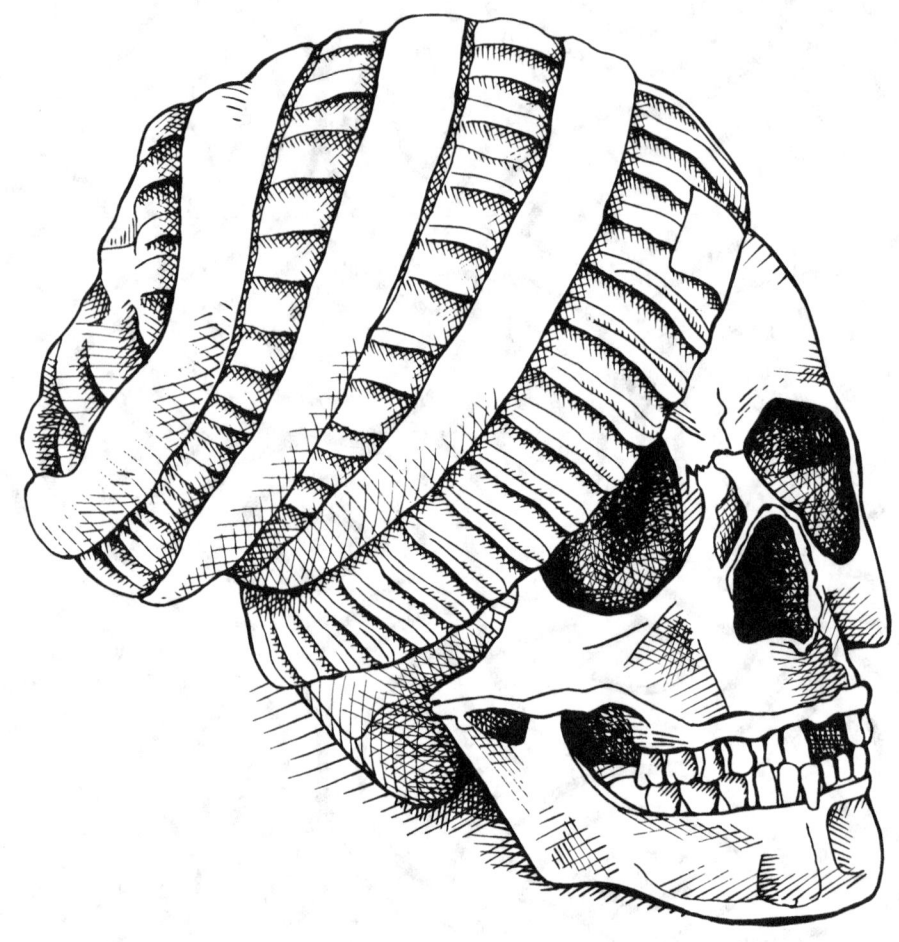

Art Therapy Adult Coloring Books

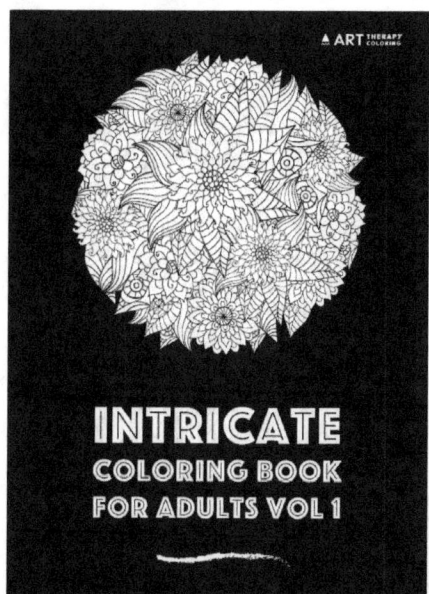

INTRICATE COLORING BOOK FOR ADULTS VOL 1

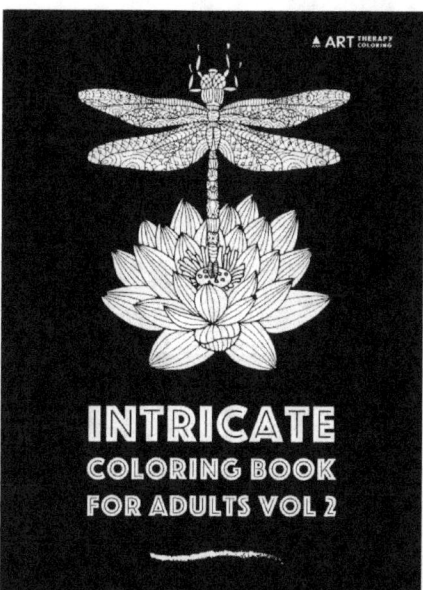

INTRICATE COLORING BOOK FOR ADULTS VOL 2

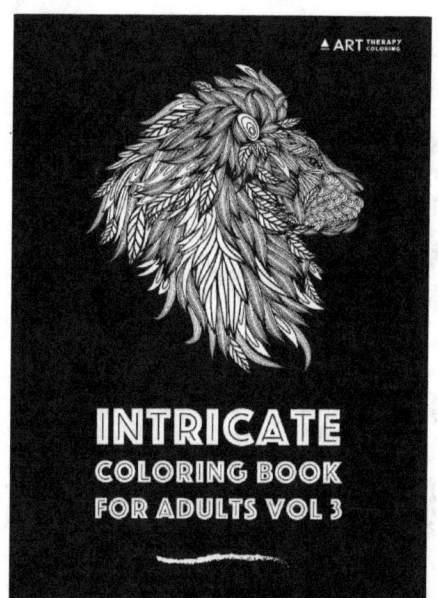

INTRICATE COLORING BOOK FOR ADULTS VOL 3

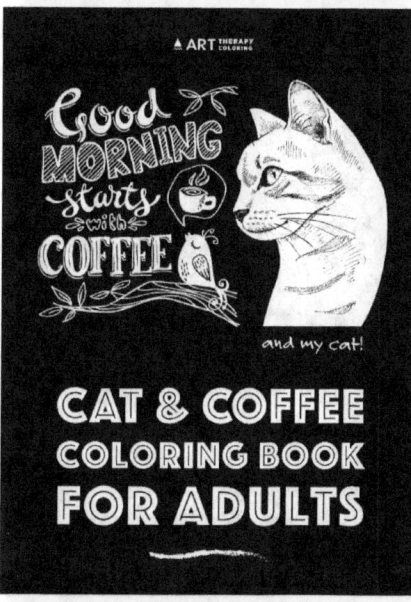

CAT & COFFEE COLORING BOOK FOR ADULTS

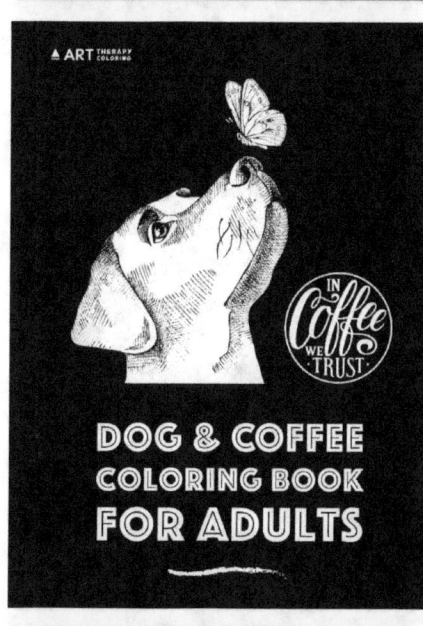

DOG & COFFEE COLORING BOOK FOR ADULTS

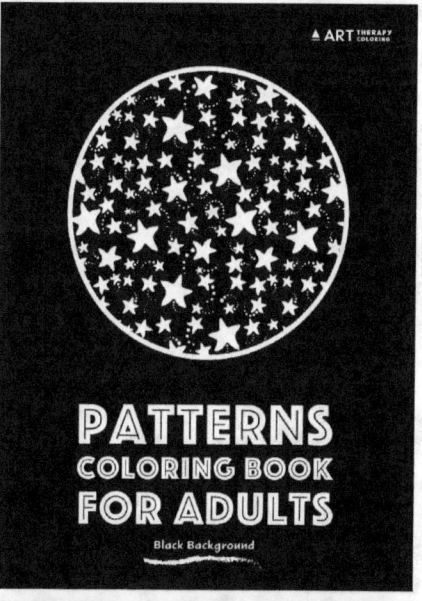

PATTERNS COLORING BOOK FOR ADULTS
Black Background

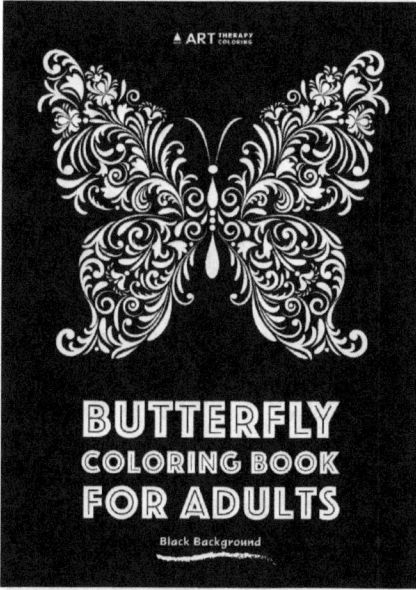

BUTTERFLY COLORING BOOK FOR ADULTS
Black Background

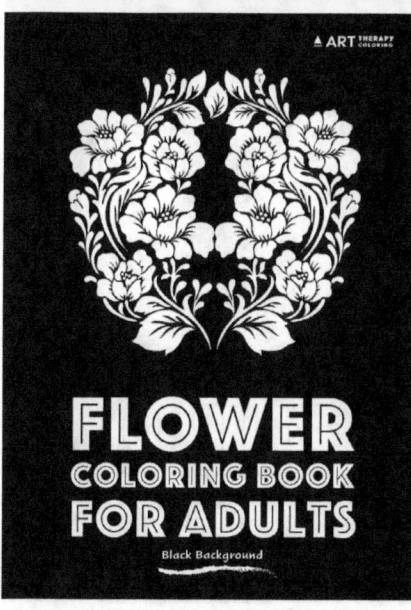

FLOWER COLORING BOOK FOR ADULTS
Black Background

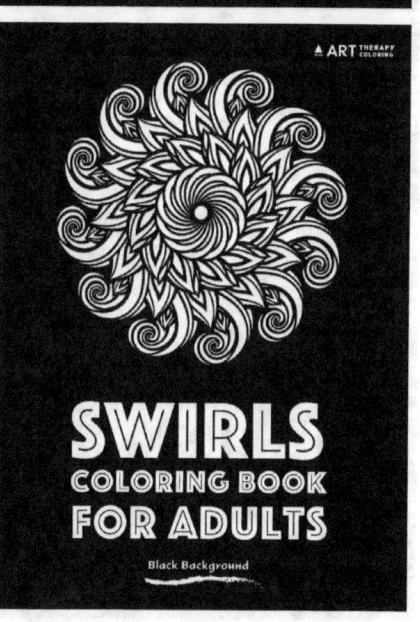

SWIRLS COLORING BOOK FOR ADULTS
Black Background

www.arttherapycoloring.com

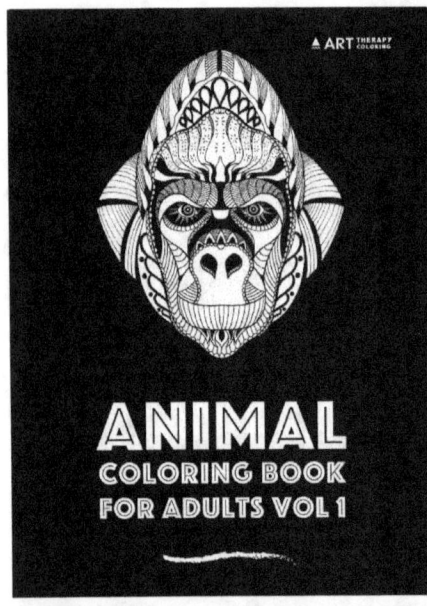

ANIMAL
COLORING BOOK
FOR ADULTS VOL 1

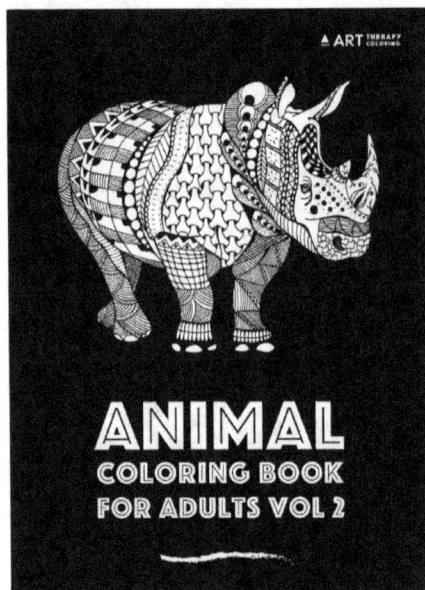

ANIMAL
COLORING BOOK
FOR ADULTS VOL 2

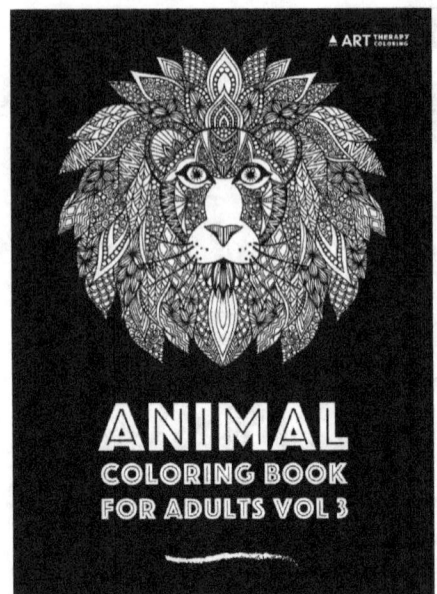

ANIMAL
COLORING BOOK
FOR ADULTS VOL 3

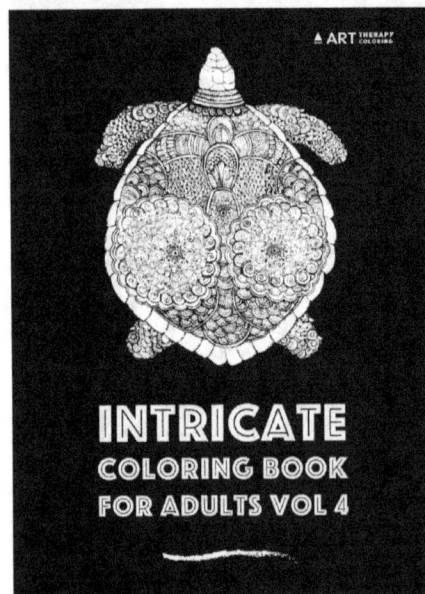

INTRICATE
COLORING BOOK
FOR ADULTS VOL 4

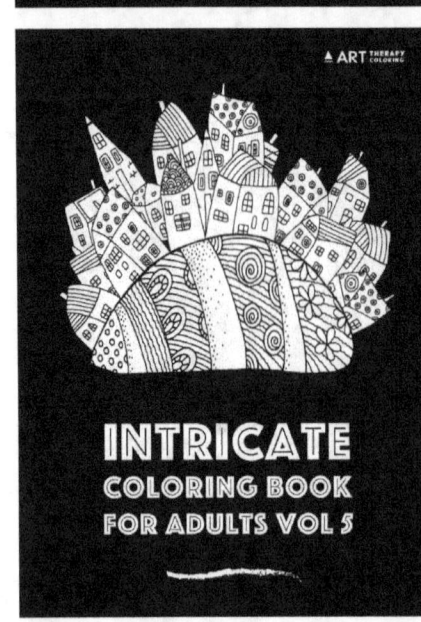

INTRICATE
COLORING BOOK
FOR ADULTS VOL 5

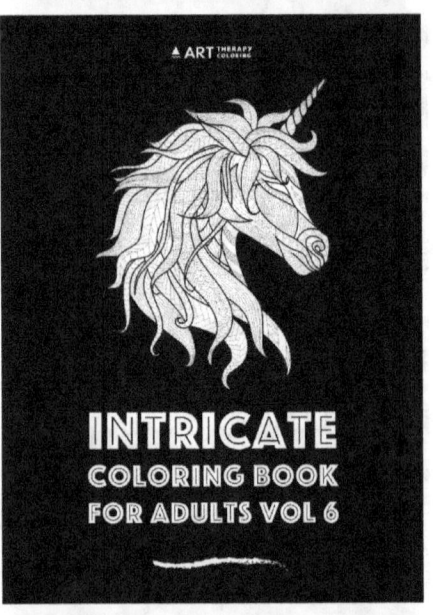

INTRICATE
COLORING BOOK
FOR ADULTS VOL 6

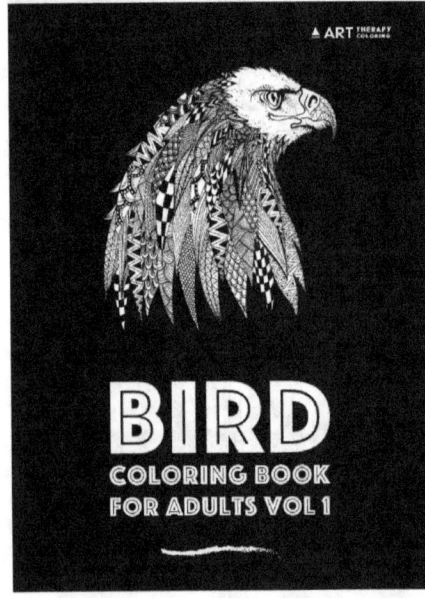

BIRD
COLORING BOOK
FOR ADULTS VOL 1

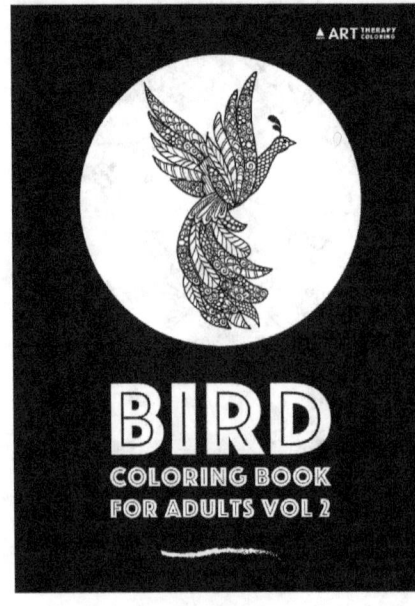

BIRD
COLORING BOOK
FOR ADULTS VOL 2

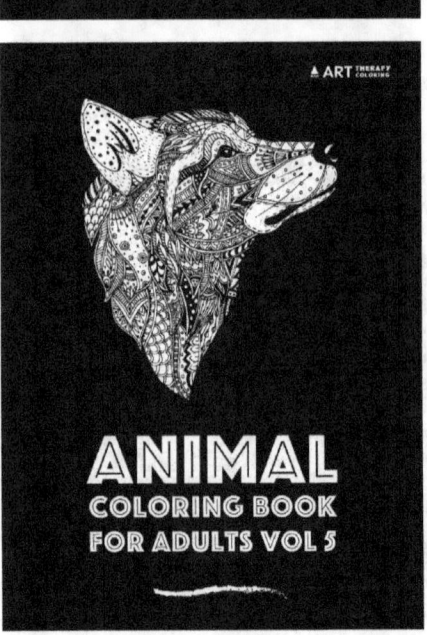

ANIMAL
COLORING BOOK
FOR ADULTS VOL 5

Art Therapy Adult Coloring Books

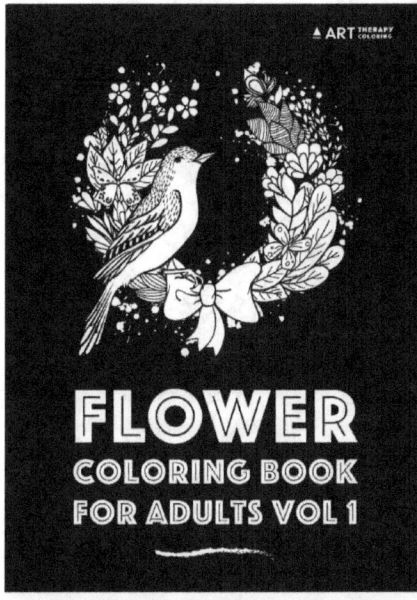

FLOWER
COLORING BOOK
FOR ADULTS VOL 1

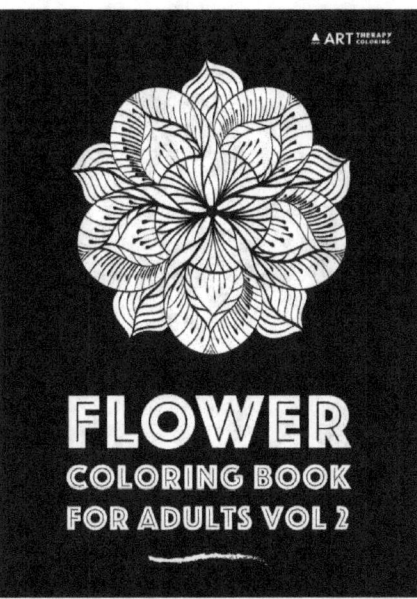

FLOWER
COLORING BOOK
FOR ADULTS VOL 2

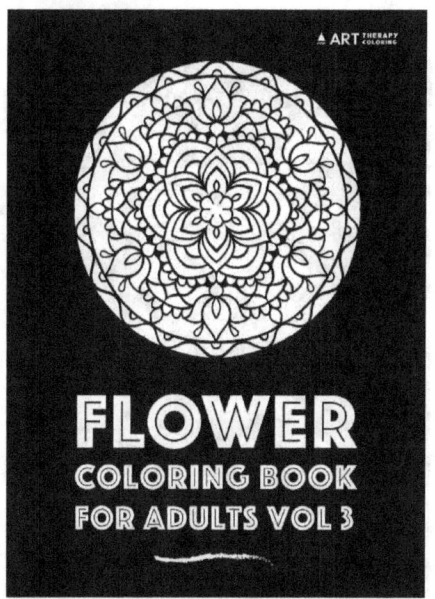

FLOWER
COLORING BOOK
FOR ADULTS VOL 3

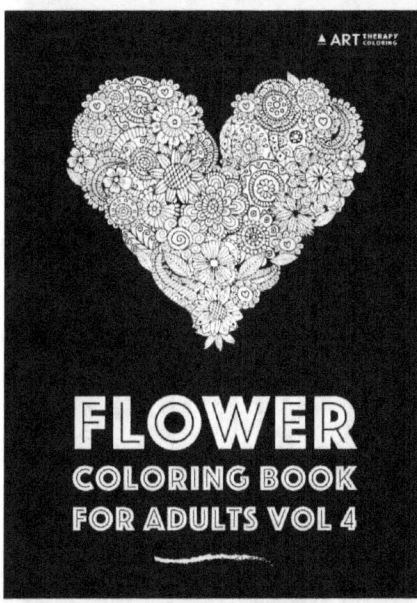

FLOWER
COLORING BOOK
FOR ADULTS VOL 4

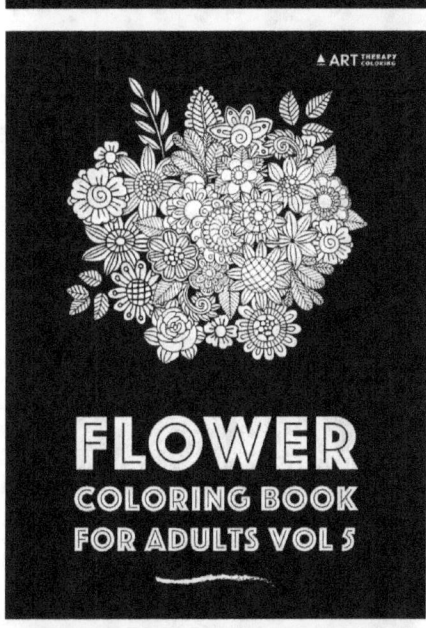

FLOWER
COLORING BOOK
FOR ADULTS VOL 5

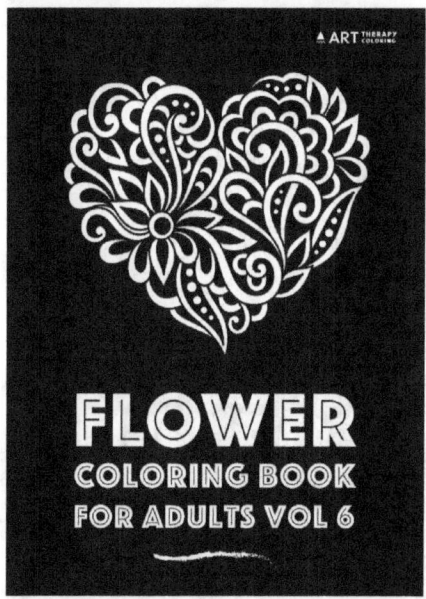

FLOWER
COLORING BOOK
FOR ADULTS VOL 6

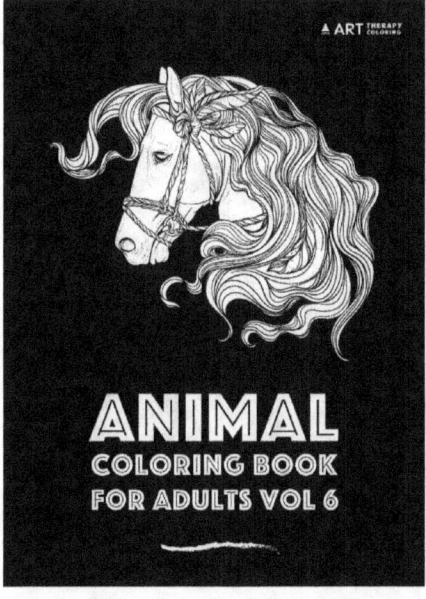

ANIMAL
COLORING BOOK
FOR ADULTS VOL 6

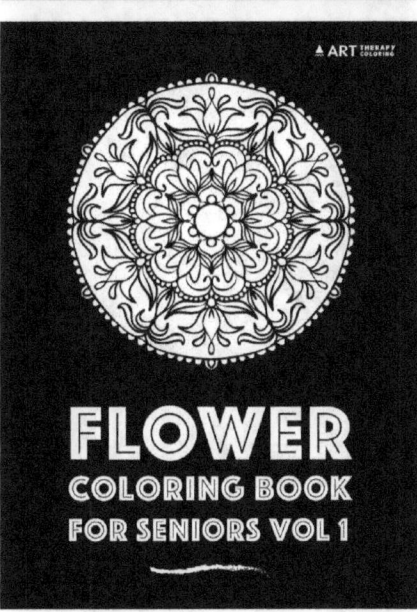

FLOWER
COLORING BOOK
FOR SENIORS VOL 1

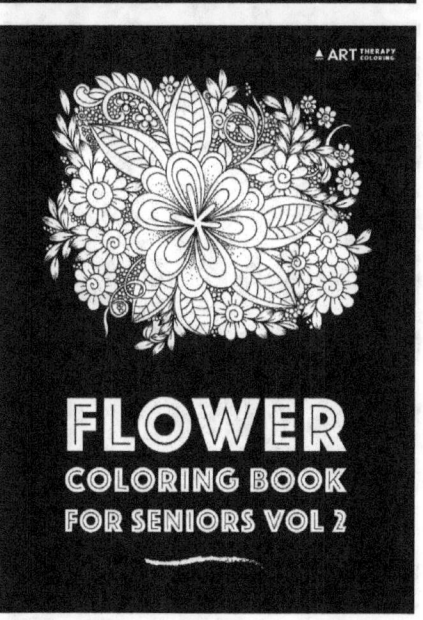

FLOWER
COLORING BOOK
FOR SENIORS VOL 2

www.arttherapycoloring.com

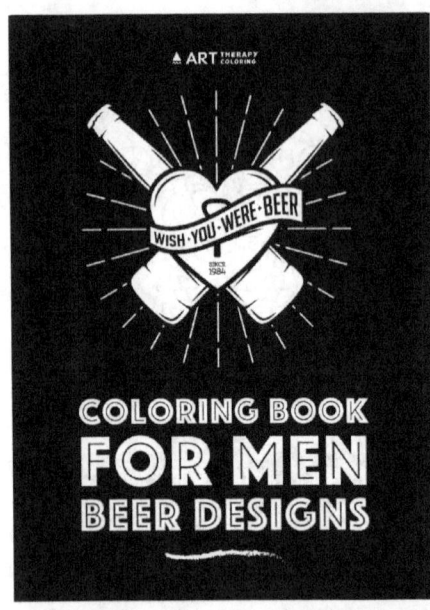

COLORING BOOK
FOR MEN
BEER DESIGNS

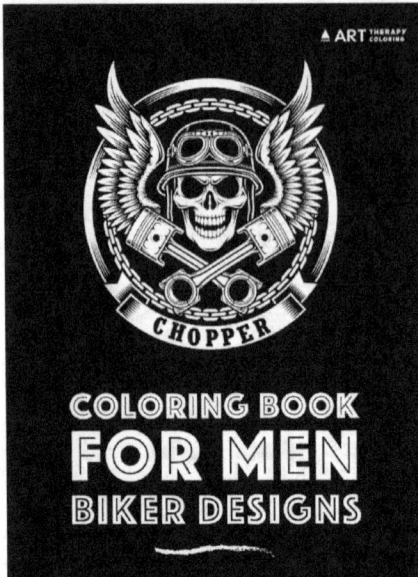

COLORING BOOK
FOR MEN
BIKER DESIGNS

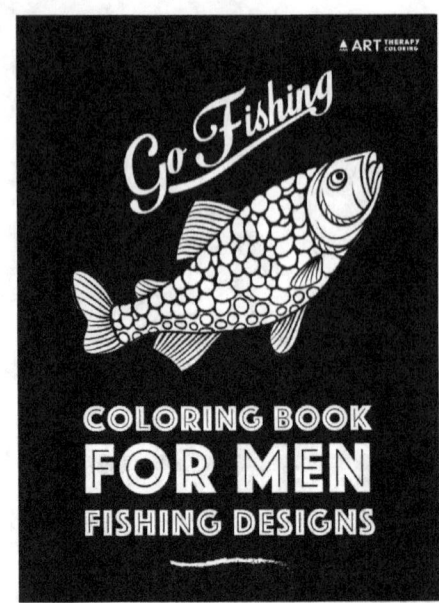

COLORING BOOK
FOR MEN
FISHING DESIGNS

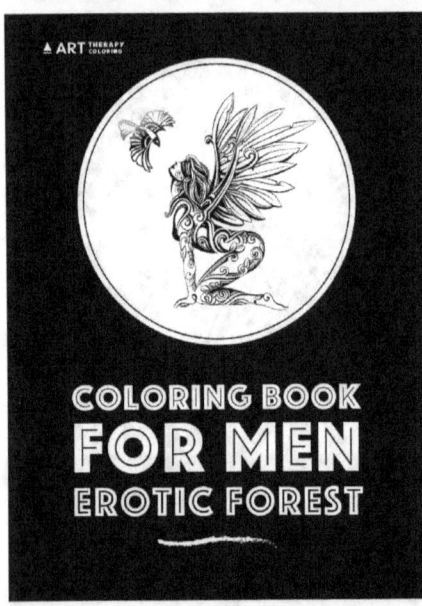

COLORING BOOK
FOR MEN
EROTIC FOREST

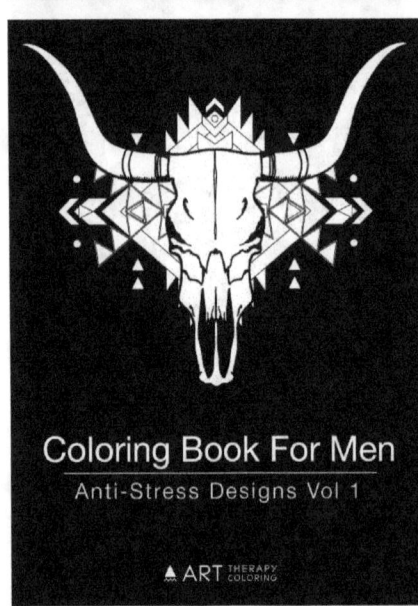

Coloring Book For Men
Anti-Stress Designs Vol 1

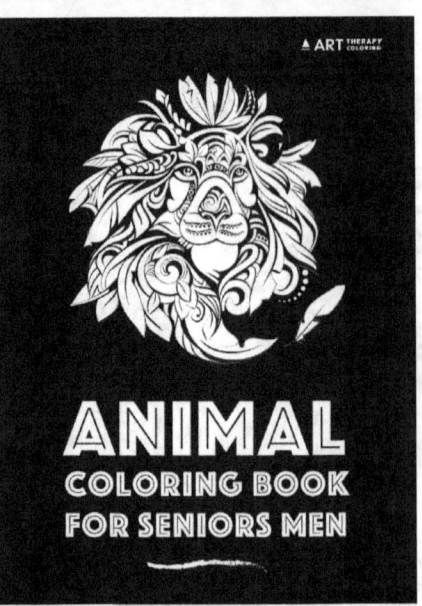

ANIMAL
COLORING BOOK
FOR SENIORS MEN

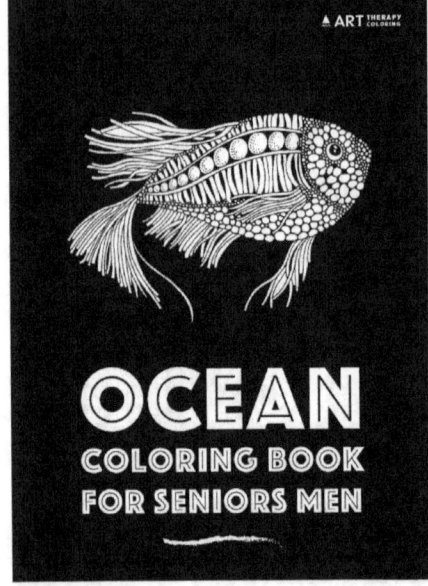

OCEAN
COLORING BOOK
FOR SENIORS MEN

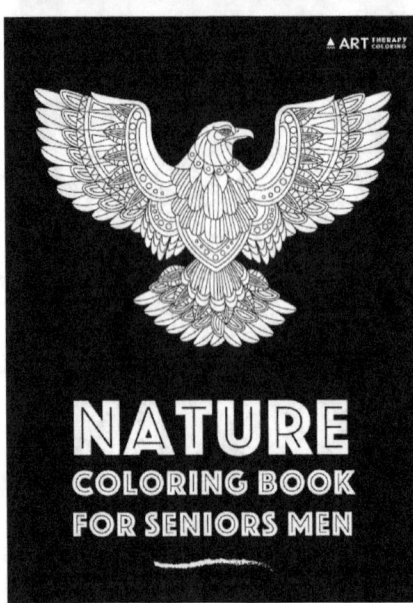

NATURE
COLORING BOOK
FOR SENIORS MEN

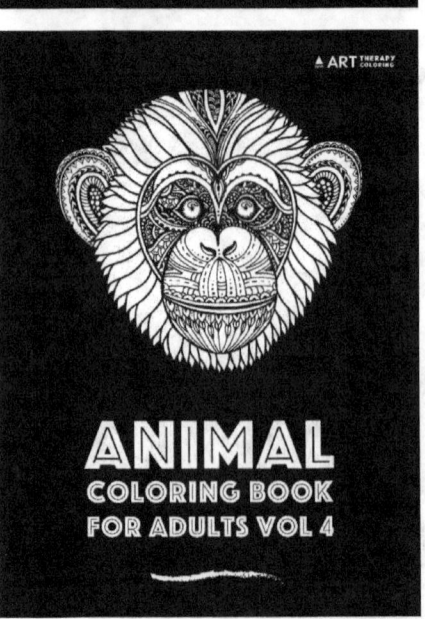

ANIMAL
COLORING BOOK
FOR ADULTS VOL 4

Art Therapy Coloring Books For Seniors

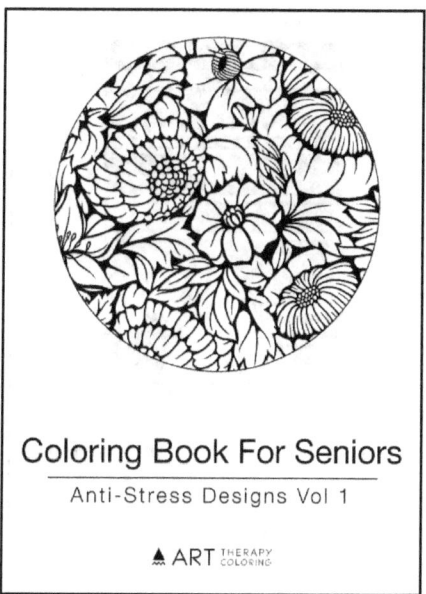

Coloring Book For Seniors
Anti-Stress Designs Vol 1

ART THERAPY COLORING

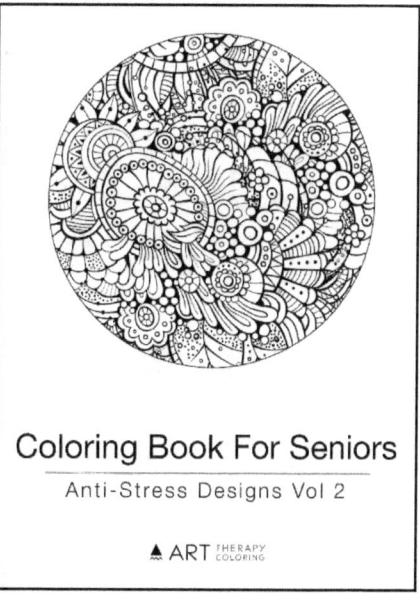

Coloring Book For Seniors
Anti-Stress Designs Vol 2

ART THERAPY COLORING

Coloring Book For Seniors
Anti-Stress Designs Vol 3

ART THERAPY COLORING

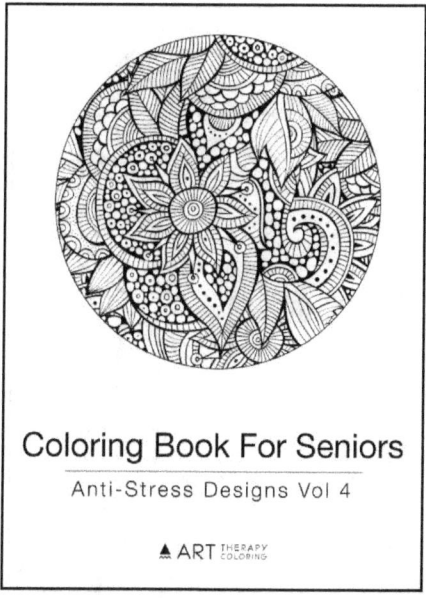

Coloring Book For Seniors
Anti-Stress Designs Vol 4

ART THERAPY COLORING

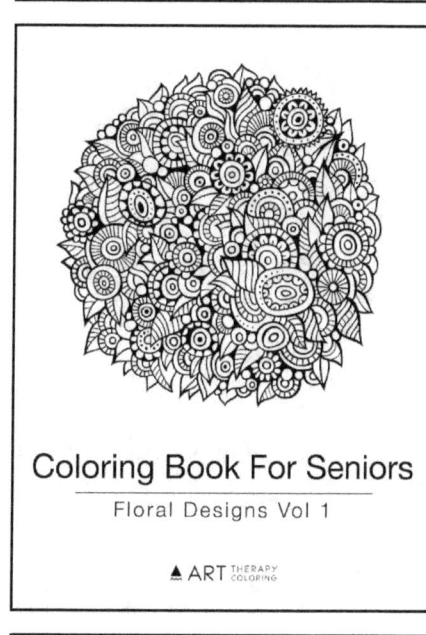

Coloring Book For Seniors
Floral Designs Vol 1

ART THERAPY COLORING

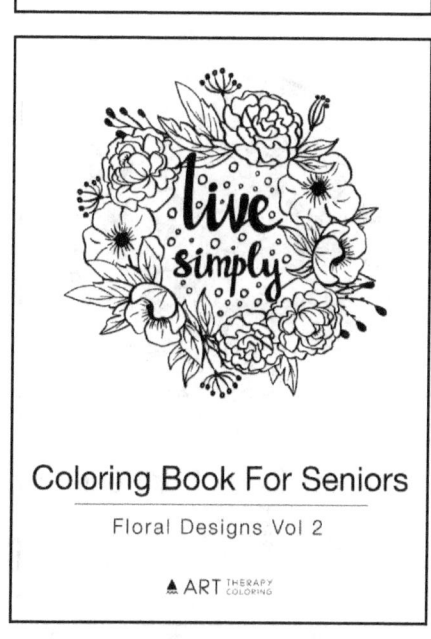

Coloring Book For Seniors
Floral Designs Vol 2

ART THERAPY COLORING

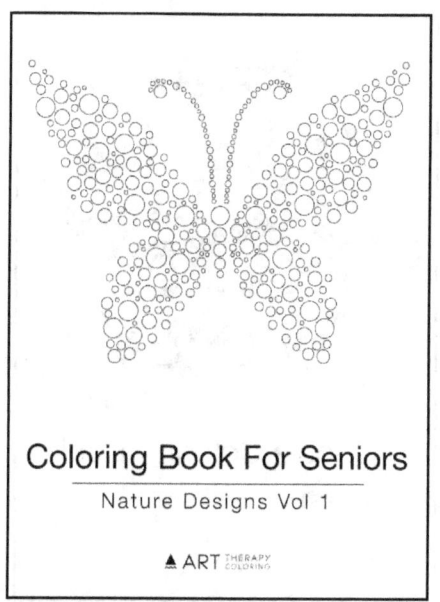

Coloring Book For Seniors
Nature Designs Vol 1

ART THERAPY COLORING

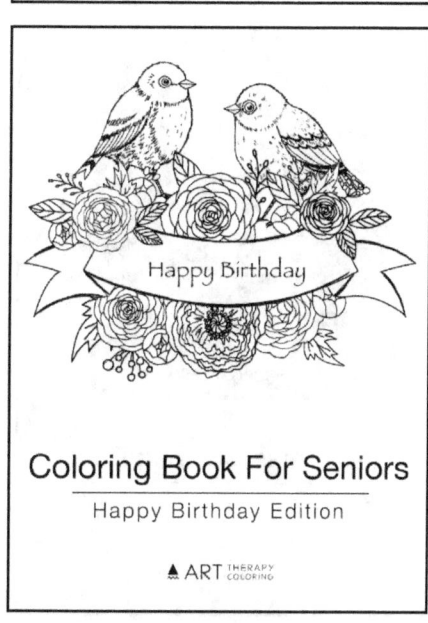

Coloring Book For Seniors
Happy Birthday Edition

ART THERAPY COLORING

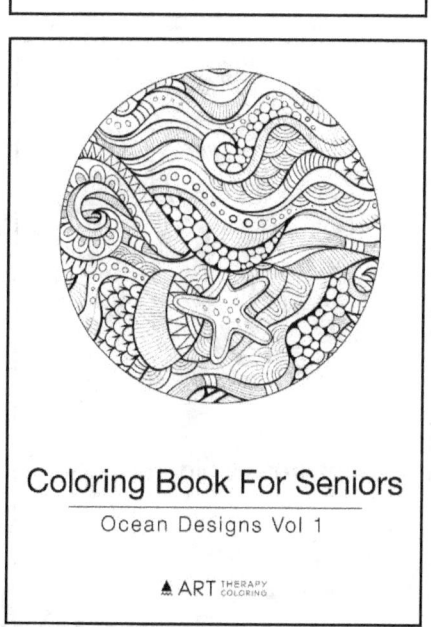

Coloring Book For Seniors
Ocean Designs Vol 1

ART THERAPY COLORING

www.arttherapycoloring.com

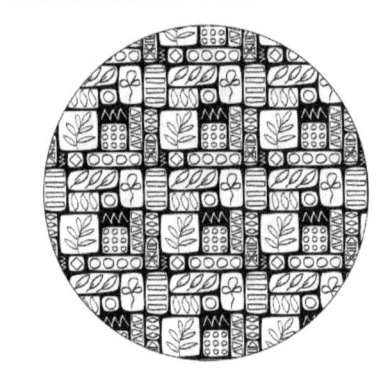

Coloring Book For Seniors
Geometric Designs Vol 1

ART THERAPY COLORING

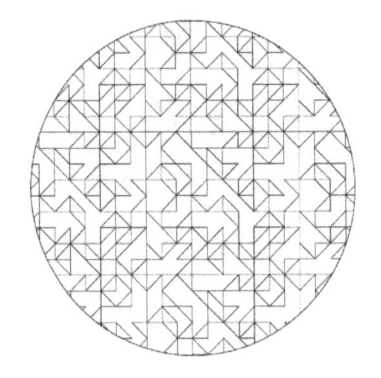

Coloring Book For Seniors
Geometric Designs Vol 2

ART THERAPY COLORING

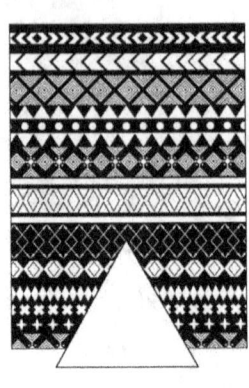

Coloring Book For Seniors
Geometric Designs Vol 3

ART THERAPY COLORING

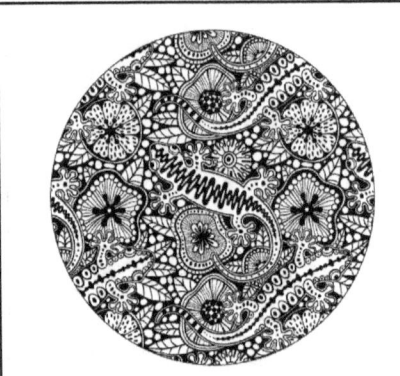

Coloring Book For Seniors
Nature Designs Vol 2

ART THERAPY COLORING

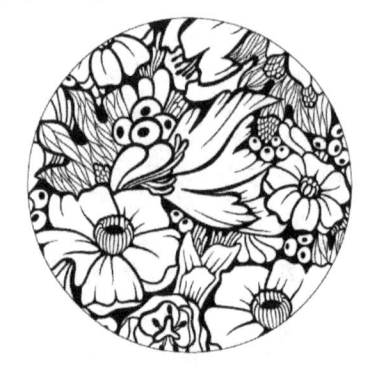

Anti-Stress Coloring Book
Stress Relieving Designs Vol 1

ART THERAPY COLORING

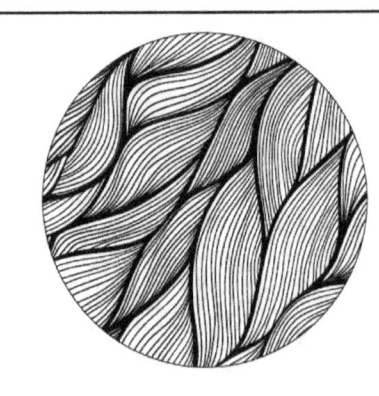

Anti-Stress Coloring Book
Stress Relieving Designs Vol 2

ART THERAPY COLORING

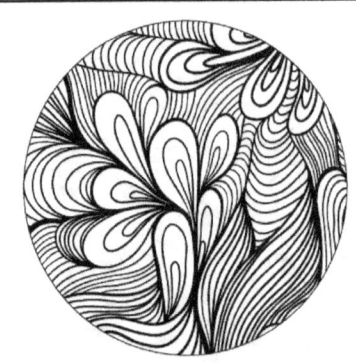

Anti-Stress Coloring Book
Stress Relieving Designs Vol 3

ART THERAPY COLORING

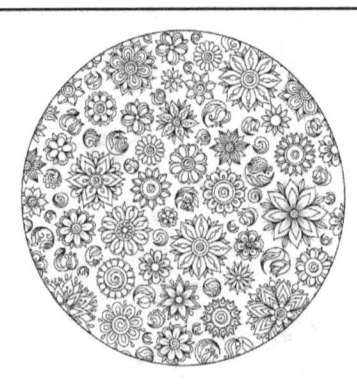

Anti-Stress Coloring Book
Stress Relieving Designs Vol 4

ART THERAPY COLORING

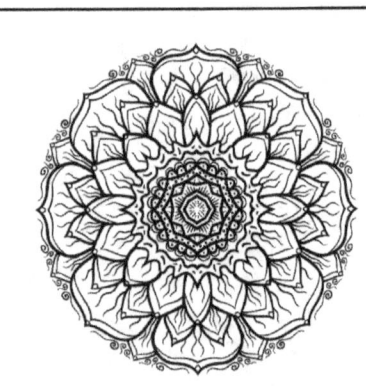

Mandala Coloring Book
Stress Relieving Designs Vol 1

ART THERAPY COLORING

Art Therapy Adult Coloring Books

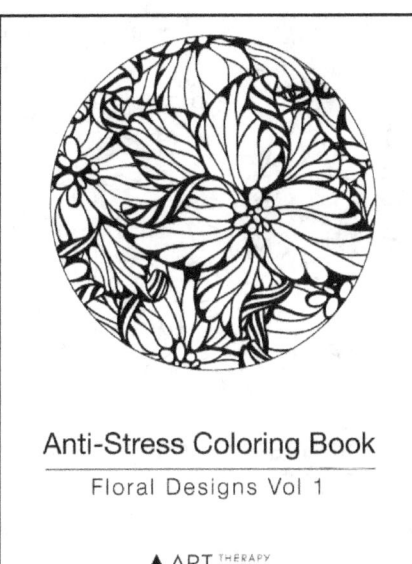

Anti-Stress Coloring Book
Floral Designs Vol 1

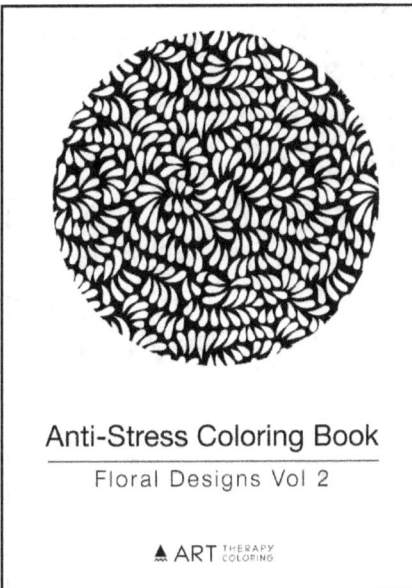

Anti-Stress Coloring Book
Floral Designs Vol 2

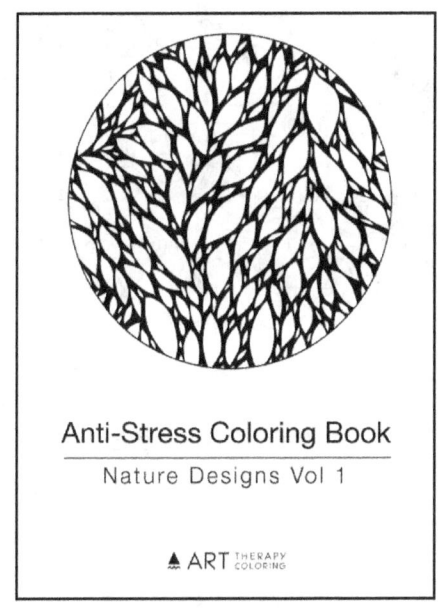

Anti-Stress Coloring Book
Nature Designs Vol 1

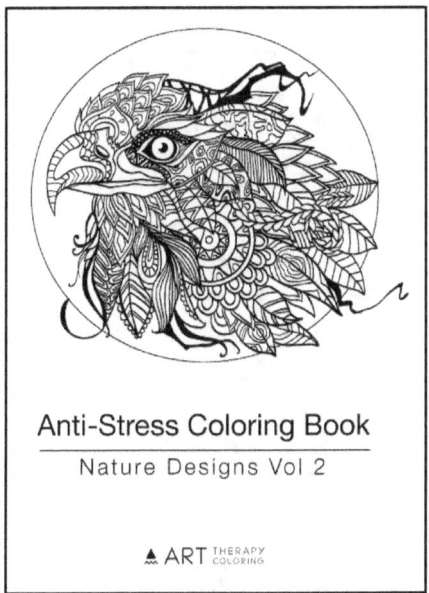

Anti-Stress Coloring Book
Nature Designs Vol 2

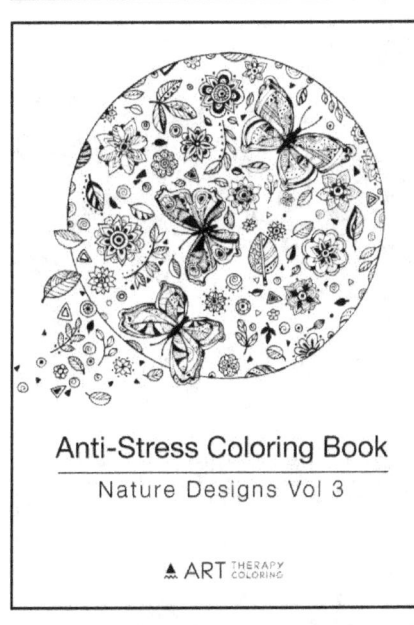

Anti-Stress Coloring Book
Nature Designs Vol 3

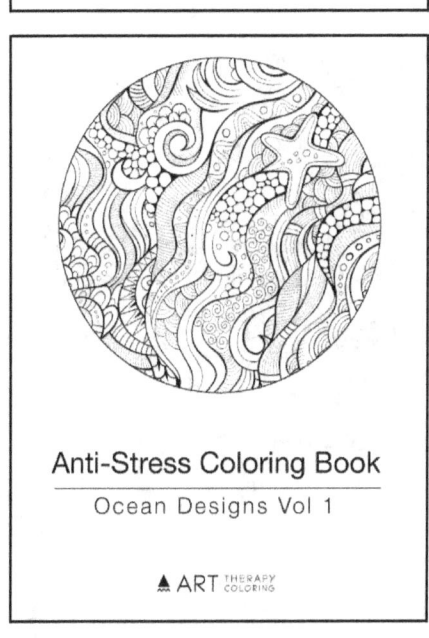

Anti-Stress Coloring Book
Ocean Designs Vol 1

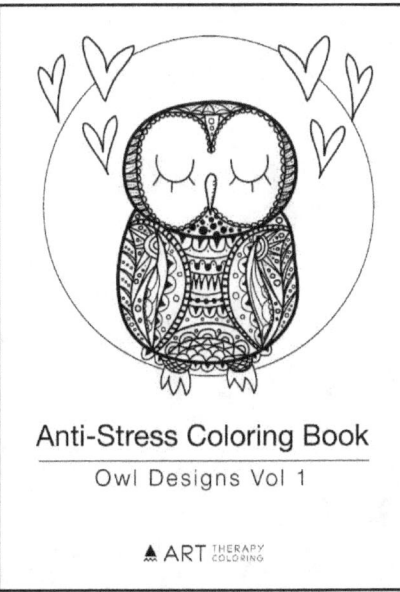

Anti-Stress Coloring Book
Owl Designs Vol 1

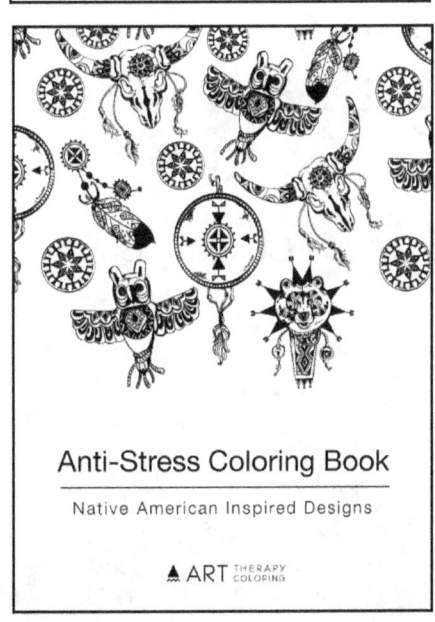

Anti-Stress Coloring Book
Native American Inspired Designs

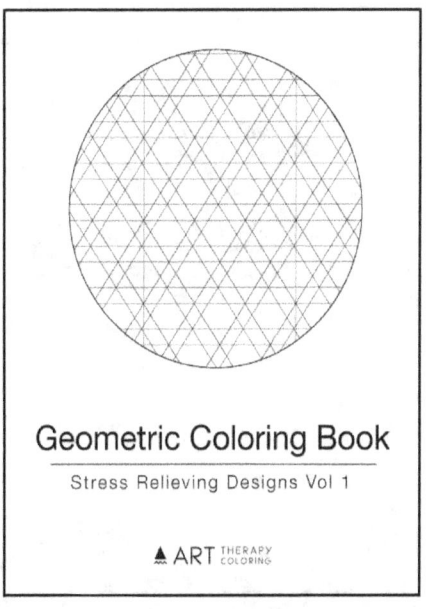

Geometric Coloring Book
Stress Relieving Designs Vol 1

www.arttherapycoloring.com

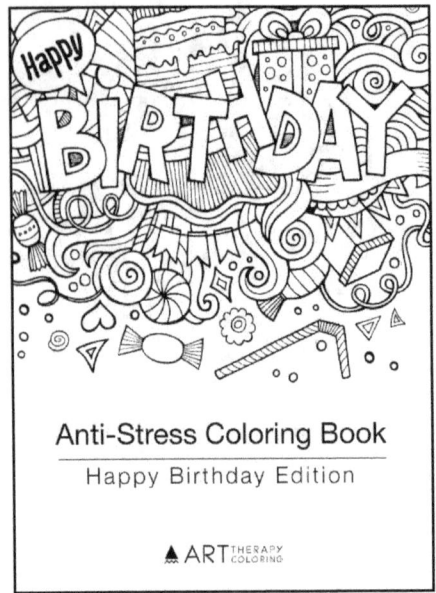

Anti-Stress Coloring Book
Happy Birthday Edition

ART THERAPY COLORING

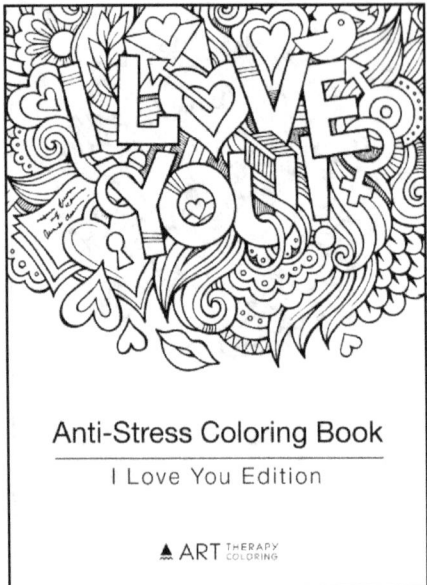

Anti-Stress Coloring Book
I Love You Edition

ART THERAPY COLORING

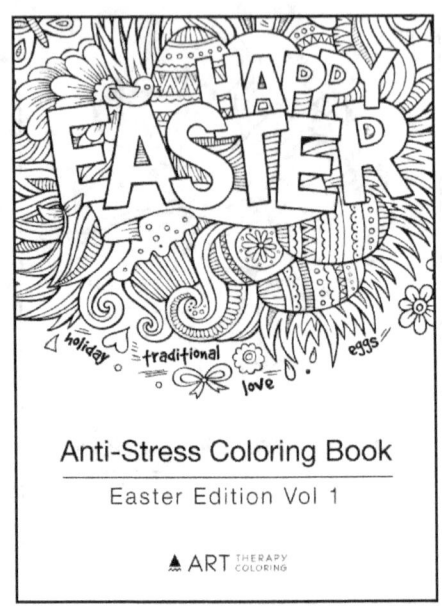

Anti-Stress Coloring Book
Easter Edition Vol 1

ART THERAPY COLORING

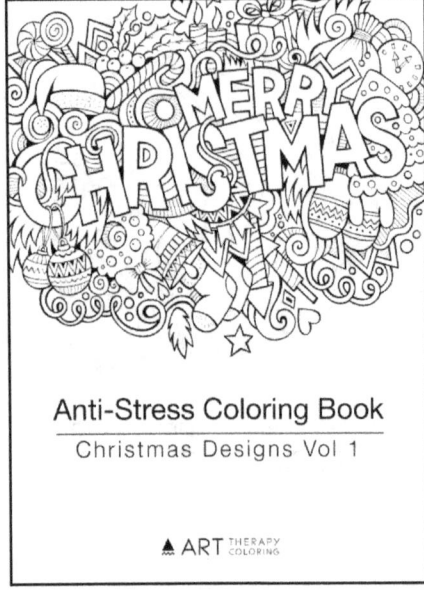

Anti-Stress Coloring Book
Christmas Designs Vol 1

ART THERAPY COLORING

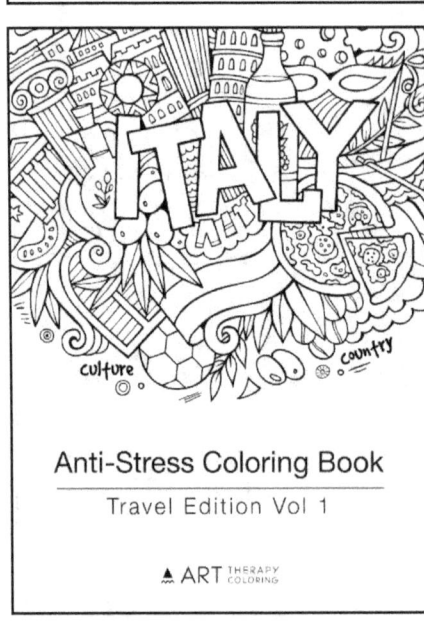

Anti-Stress Coloring Book
Travel Edition Vol 1

ART THERAPY COLORING

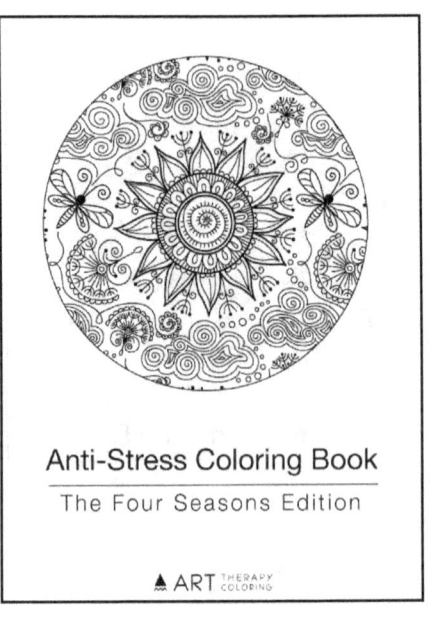

Anti-Stress Coloring Book
The Four Seasons Edition

ART THERAPY COLORING

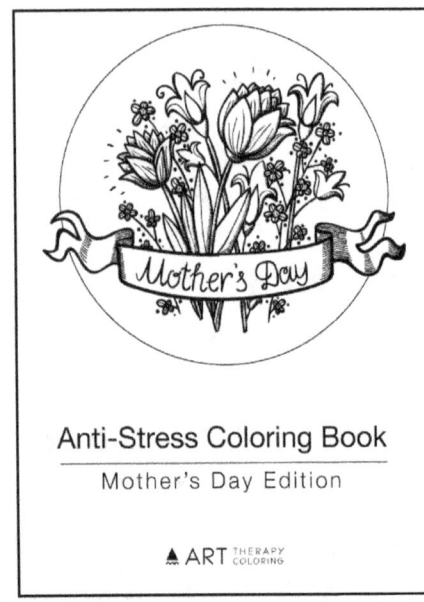

Anti-Stress Coloring Book
Mother's Day Edition

ART THERAPY COLORING

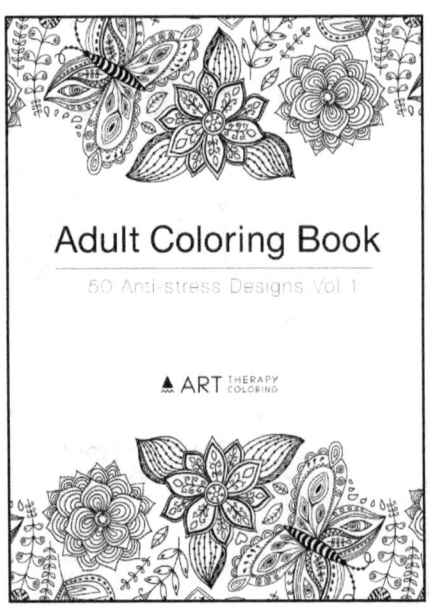

Adult Coloring Book
50 Anti-stress Designs Vol 1

ART THERAPY COLORING

Art Therapy Coloring Books For Teens

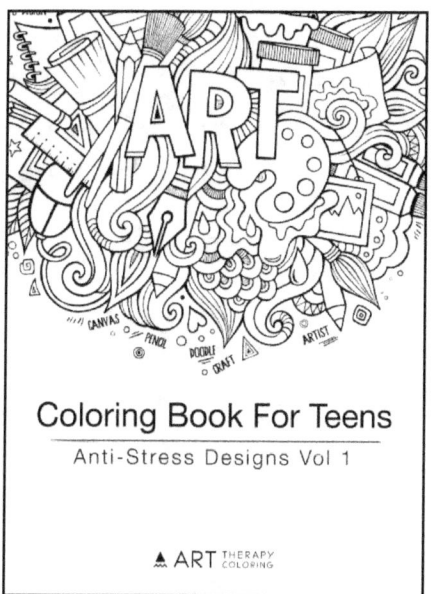

Coloring Book For Teens
Anti-Stress Designs Vol 1

▲ ART THERAPY COLORING

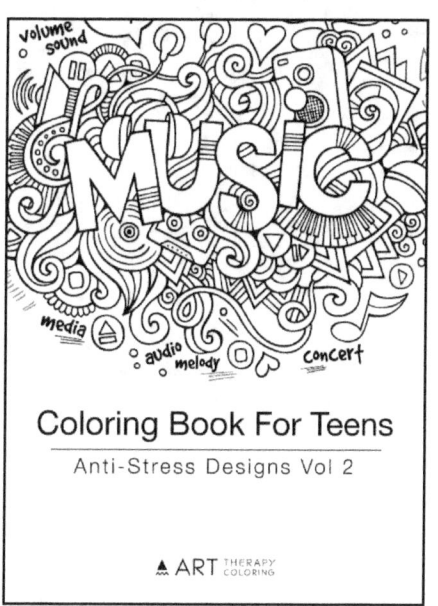

Coloring Book For Teens
Anti-Stress Designs Vol 2

▲ ART THERAPY COLORING

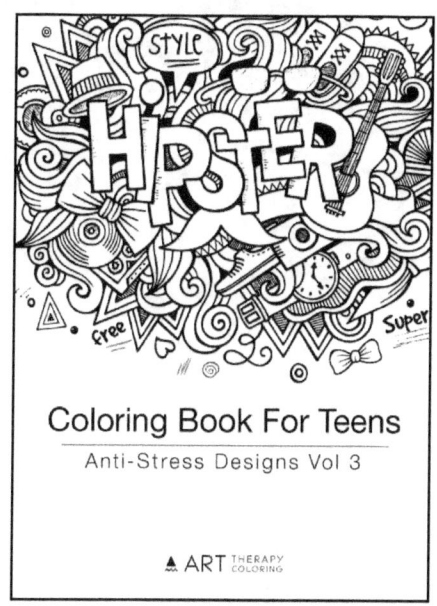

Coloring Book For Teens
Anti-Stress Designs Vol 3

▲ ART THERAPY COLORING

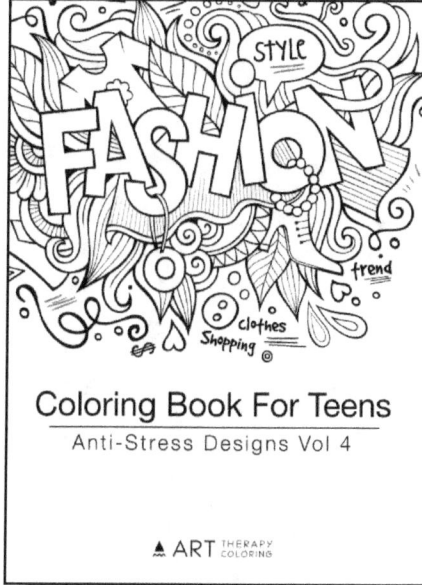

Coloring Book For Teens
Anti-Stress Designs Vol 4

▲ ART THERAPY COLORING

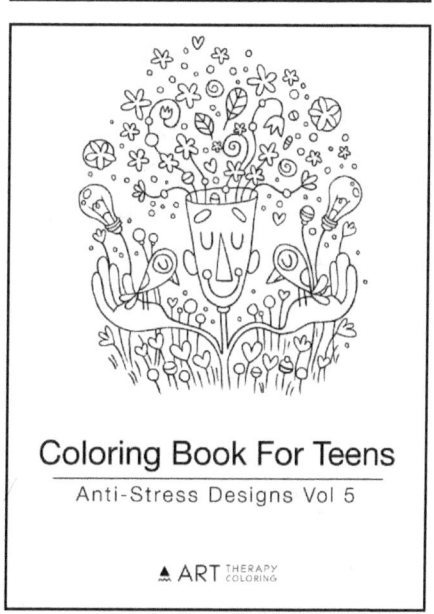

Coloring Book For Teens
Anti-Stress Designs Vol 5

▲ ART THERAPY COLORING

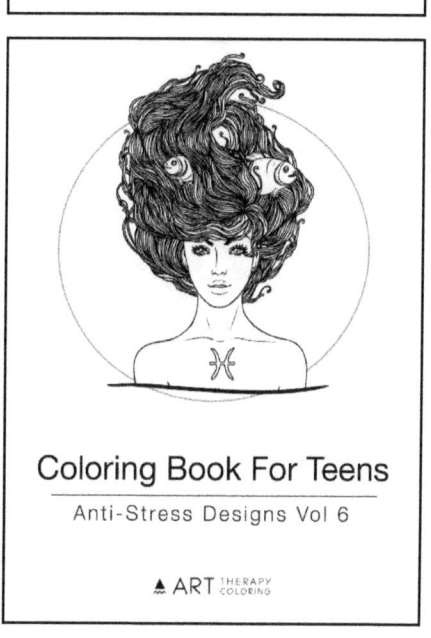

Coloring Book For Teens
Anti-Stress Designs Vol 6

▲ ART THERAPY COLORING

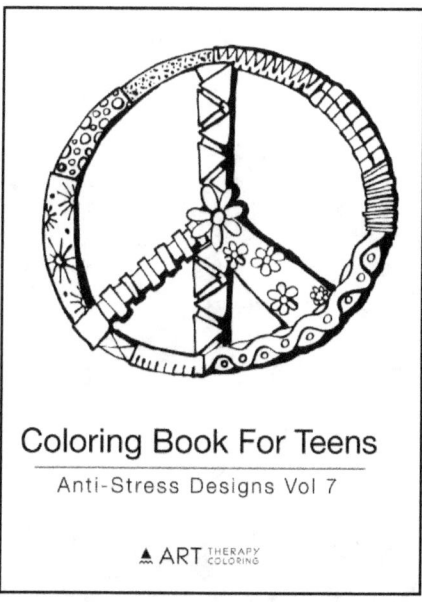

Coloring Book For Teens
Anti-Stress Designs Vol 7

▲ ART THERAPY COLORING

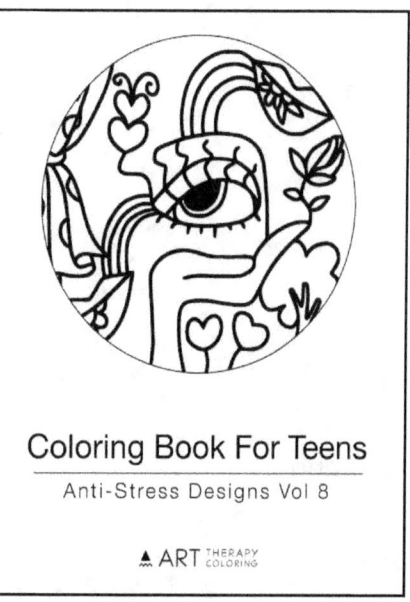

Coloring Book For Teens
Anti-Stress Designs Vol 8

▲ ART THERAPY COLORING

Ocean Coloring Book
For Seniors Men

Published by:
Art Therapy Coloring
El Dorado Hills, California
www.arttherapycoloring.com

ISBN: 978-1-944427-74-0

www.ingramcontent.com/pod-product-compliance
Lightning Source LLC
Chambersburg PA
CBHW081611220526
45468CB00010B/2844